Creative  Stained Glass

Techniques for Unfired and Fired Projects

by POLLY ROTHENBERG

CROWN PUBLISHERS, INC., NEW YORK

*Inquiries should
be addressed to Crown Publishers, Inc.,
419 Park Avenue South, New York, N.Y. 10016*

*Library of Congress Catalog Card Number: 73–82930
Printed in the United States of America*

*Published simultaneously in Canada by
General Publishing Company Limited*

Designed by Shari de Miskey

Fourth Printing, September, 1975

*All stained glass projects are demonstrated by
Polly Rothenberg.*

Contents

Preface

FOR CENTURIES stained glass has richly adorned the churches of the world, uplifting the spirits of millions of worshippers. Except for brief historical interludes when stained glass was used in private dwellings, it has been associated almost entirely with religious architecture. Today, the classical art of designing with this beautiful transparent material has swept aside the last restraints of its ancient ecclesiastical role. Stained glass has moved into the modern world of secular architecture and home workshop creations. With new attitudes and new methods of utilizing the vibrant beauty of its colors, enthusiastic craftsmen are creating delightful stained glass panels, windows, lanterns, jewelry, whimsical hangings, small sculptures, and countless accessories even during the basic learning involvement. Simple shapes become alive the moment they capture a gleam of sunshine. Moving daylight sends its rays through each bit of glass in ever-changing hues. Projects planned to display their colors indoors at night need only a simple installation of artificial backlighting to continue casting an iridescent spell.

Anyone who loves color and beauty can learn how to create attractive stained glass objects by following easy-to-learn but precise directions. The illustrated step-by-step instructions in this book offer both simple and complex projects that are fun to follow. As skill and confidence develop, your own creativity and initiative will emerge. Once you have conquered the processes, you can develop freely many unusual and creative ideas of your own.

Stained glass lantern made of antique glass, 20″ tall, 10″ in diameter. Bette Warner.

Fused laminated glass hanging. R. Bruce Laughlin.

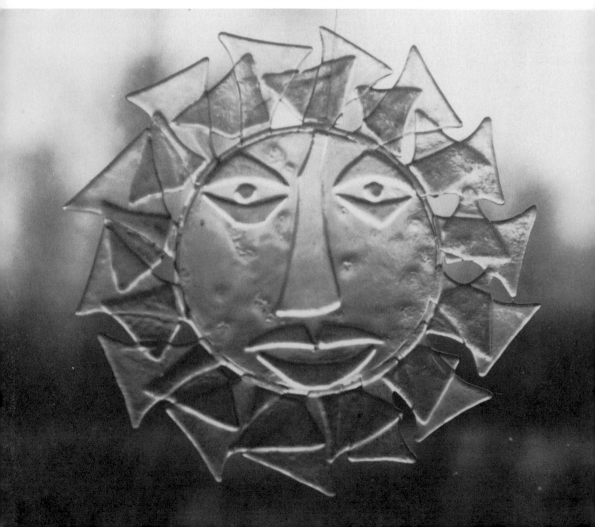

I * Introduction

Kinds of Stained Glass

ANTIQUE STAINED GLASS is the costliest and most exciting of the colored glasses. Spectacular stained glass church windows, panels, and windows in public and private buildings, and charming functional and decorative art objects are fashioned from this handmade glass. Despite its name, it is not old glass; but it is made in nearly the same way glass was formed by early glassmakers. Skilled craftsmen employ simple tools and methods to produce hand-formed sheet glass in hundreds of new colors developed by modern chemistry. Antique glass has random streaks, ripples, undulations, bubbles, or other irregularities whose seeming imperfections catch light transmitted through them to bring character and beauty to your work. Areas of preferred thicknesses in this glass are cut and sold from larger sheets, which results in a considerable waste or "curious" glass, sometimes sold by glass supply stores at a discount. This scrap sheet glass is useful for projects in basic glasscraft. Although it may not fit easily into a large leaded glass composition, it is suitable for bonding with epoxy resin, for grouted projects, and for jewelry, mobiles, and other small decorative hangings.

FLASHED STAINED GLASS denotes a variety of antique with a light-colored glass base and thinner skins of rich, more deeply contrasting colored glass. By examining the edges of a piece of flashed glass, you can see these separate color layers. Light passing through flashed glass mixes the separate color effects much the way a painter mixes his pigments. Flashed glass is useful in any project where it will not be transformed by heat: etched glass, glass bonded with epoxy resin, lead came projects, or combinations of these methods. If this glass is fired, the thin layer of colored glass will likely pull back from the edges, leaving a colorless or white rim around the glass piece. Flashed glass should be *cut* on the unflashed side, but *etched* on the flashed side.

CATHEDRAL GLASS is a machine-rolled stained glass with medium to heavy texture on one side and a smooth surface on the other. It is passed between rollers that impress a variety of textures on it while the glass is still hot and pliable. Because the glass is generally of uniform thickness of ⅛″, there is less waste than from cutting antique. It is sold in a wide variety of delightful colors and textures. Rolled patterns in this glass are called hammered, rippled, seedy (containing tiny bubbles), antique texture, and Marine antique, a rolled glass in light clear colors. Cathedral glass is cut on the smooth side.

SLAB GLASS (DALLES) is the name given to an extra-clear colored antique glass cast in thick slabs. These slabs are generally 8″ x 12″, or 12″ x 12″; They may vary from ½″ to 1″ in thickness. A steel wedge, a dalle-cutting hammer, and special skills are required to cut these extra-thick slabs. But the novice can make wonderful projects with broken segments of this glass. An unusual cutting procedure, called *faceting*, gives them reflective sparkle and leaves a myriad of small thick glass chips which have many decorative uses. Most glass suppliers sell broken slab glass segments.

RONDELS are round disks of antique glass made by blowing a bubble, then twirling the hot molten glass bubble on the end of the blowing rod to flatten it by centrifugal force. Rondels are made in many sizes and colors. These very decorative forms are useful in leaded and bonded compositions.

JEWELS are small novelty stained glass forms used decoratively either singly or as part of a larger composition. They are especially effective when they are bonded or leaded into glass lamps and lanterns, or when made into jewelry.

Cutting the Glass

Although your first project may be confined to compositions made from glass scraps, you will find random glass shapes that can be improved by a little nipping and cutting here and there as you visualize how you can combine them into attractive designs. "Cutting" glass is a term that does not adequately describe the process. When glass is scored with a tiny sharp metal wheel set into a wooden- or metal-handled cutter, only the surface of the glass is fractured. The cut encourages glass molecules to open up along the scored line *when adequate pressure is applied*. Amazingly, this pressure must be applied at once, if you would make a clean separation. If more than a couple of minutes elapse, the separated molecules of glass will "close ranks" so that a clean separation is not achieved, even though the scored line is still visible. This characteristic of glass is unknown to the average novice. It may explain why a clean scored line does not always result in a clean separation of the glass when you are first learning to cut it.

Certain safety precautions must be followed when you work with glass. Always wear gloves (suede finish gloves are fine) when you transport large sheets of glass. Keep glass bins on the floor so you do not have to elevate the glass over your head; it may have fine cracks and suddenly break as you move it. Do not grab at a falling sheet of glass; the reason is obvious. Let it fall. Avoid the dangerous hazard involved in attempting to work with or transport glass over another person's head or body. Never carry a piece of glass with the edge resting against the web of skin between your thumb and forefinger; it can be gashed. If a choice piece of glass is partially buried beneath other pieces of glass, remove the upper glass, starting from the top. If you try to shuffle the glass around with bare hands, you are likely to receive multiple gashes. Always sand or scrape the edges of newly cut glass to remove the razor-sharp thin slivers that often appear along a newly cut edge. The most common cause of small aggravating and painful cuts is absentmindedly brushing or pressing the bare hands on the minute glass shards which litter the worktable's cutting surface after a session of glass cutting. After receiving a few of these painful (although usually not severe) cuts, you will automatically discontinue this careless practice. Happily, very few glass craftsmen cut themselves severely.

An inexpensive glass cutter with a hard steel cutting wheel is adequate for general use and it will give long service when proper care is exercised. Carbide cutting wheels, a little more expensive, give longer service and greater separation of the glass surface when it is scored. Commercial diamonds set into cutters are costly and they are not easy for the inexperienced craftsman to control, although many professional glass craftsmen like the flexibility they provide in cutting intricate shapes. The cutters used for projects in this book have tungsten carbide cutting wheels.

The cutting table must be firm, flat, and level. To maintain good arm leverage, it is best to stand while you cut glass. The table should have a comfortable height for this standing position. About 34" to 36" from the floor is adequate worktable height for the average person. If the table is too low, your back will begin to feel the strain. A piece of short pile carpet makes a good cutting surface for the tabletop if you are cutting large shapes. Tiny slivers from glass cuttings drop into the pile where they do not interfere with subsequent cutting or scratch the glass when it is being shifted. Carpet is resilient enough to "give" under the pressure exerted to separate the glass. Remove the carpet occasionally and shake it very gently over a broad trash container to rid it of accumulated scraps of glass. Some craftsmen prefer to place a few layers of paper or a sheet of pressed cork on the cutting table instead of carpet, especially when small shapes are cut.

Although rulers or other straight edges can guide the cutter when straight lines are scored, they have the annoying propensity of shifting suddenly or sliding on the glass (especially on uneven antique stained glass). Until you become adept at glass cutting, you can control this slippage by gluing a long strip of thin rubber to the underside of the straightedge. "Rug grip," sold in carpet stores, is excellent for this purpose. Before cutting begins, clean the glass with detergent water to remove all soil that may cause the cutter to skip and make separation of the scored glass difficult or ragged. Lubricate the cutting wheel with kerosene occasionally to ensure the best service from it. The cutter can be stored in a small bottle or can partially filled with kerosene. When scoring glass, hold the cutter perpendicular to the tabletop. It can lean toward you slightly, but if it tilts sideways, one edge of the separated glass may be undercut and leave a rough edge.

To begin, place the glass on the table, smoothest side up. Dip the cutter into kerosene and dab it on a paper towel to remove excess oil. Beginning about ⅛" from the edge of the glass to avoid chipping the edge, make a firm continuous even stroke from one edge of the glass to the other edge *without pausing or lifting the cutter.* Score either toward you or away from you, whichever is easier and allows you to see where you are going. Hold the cutter close to the guiding straight-edge; it must not wander away from the straight line you are scoring. Press it firmly against the glass. It should make a soft steady scratching or rasping sound as it bites into the glass. Long even cuts against a straightedge are not automatically easy to control; they require complete concentration. If the cutter begins to lean sideways, the cutting wheel will curve away from the guide stick. Some craftsmen prefer to lay a straightedged sheet of paper under the glass and guide the cutting wheel above it. If you should hit a glass bubble, ease the cutter gently over it. Only experience can teach you how firmly pressure must be applied. In spite of a few false starts, it is surprising how quickly you will gain confidence after a session of practice on glass scraps or inexpensive window glass.

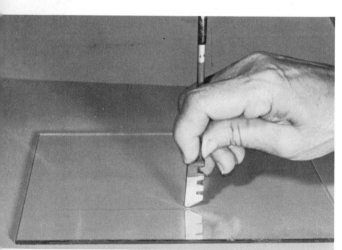

Hold the glass cutter perpendicular between your first and second fingers. The thumb supports the cutter on the underside of the flat surface just above the cutter notches. The tiny cutting wheel rides on the glass.

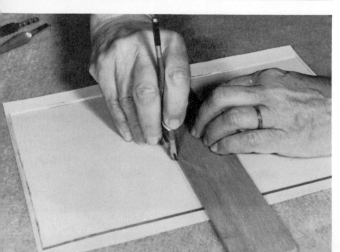

Before you start, clean the glass with liquid cleaner. Begin scoring about 1/16" from the edge of the glass and make a firm continuous even stroke without pausing or lifting the cutter. Do not retrace the stroke. Just as you reach the end of the score line, relax your hand so the cutter does not chip the glass edge.

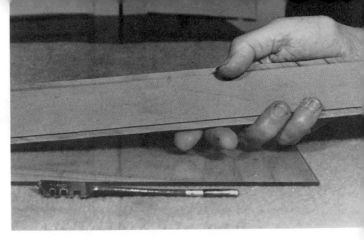

When you score straight lines along a guide stick, keep the straightedge from slipping by gluing a wide strip of thin rubber "rug grip" to the underside of the guide stick; it may be bought in rug stores.

As soon as the glass has been scored, lay the ball end of your glass cutter under the near end of the score line and immediately press firmly down with your thumbs on each side of the line at the end nearest you. The scored glass should separate evenly. If it doesn't, lay the glass over the table edge so the scored line comes just beyond and parallel to the tabletop; with one hand pressing the glass firmly against the top of the table, snap the glass in two with the other hand bending it down and away from the table. Hang onto the glass as you force it down so it does not fall suddenly to the floor; it may shatter. After these two tries, if you have not separated the glass another procedure must be tried. Hold the glass in one hand and, holding the cutter near its end in the other hand, tap firmly but gently all along the scored line underneath the glass. Tap first at one end, then the other end, and along the middle of the line. You will soon see a fracture developing under the scored line. Hold the glass over the table in case it should fall apart suddenly, which it frequently will do. Apply equal pressure to the two sides of the fractured score line and snap them apart. Long curved cuts are made the same way if they are not too sharply curved.

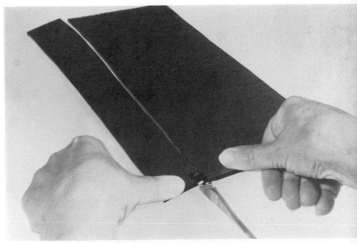

As soon as the glass has been scored, lay one end of the cutter under the near end of the score line and immediately press down firmly on each side of the line. The glass should separate evenly.

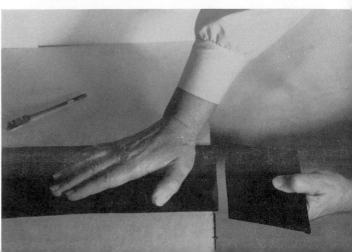

Another method of separating the glass. With one hand pressing the glass against the tabletop, and with the score line extending over the edge and parallel to it, snap the glass down and out.

Tap firmly but gently all along the scored line underneath the glass for another way to separate it. You will see a fracture developing under the scored line.

Apply equal pressure to the two sides of the fractured score line and snap them apart.

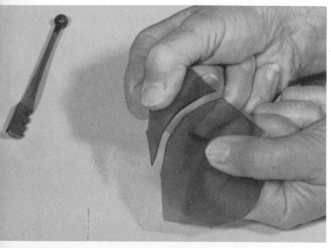

Small pieces are snapped apart on the score line with the thumbs and curled forefingers pressing down and outward.

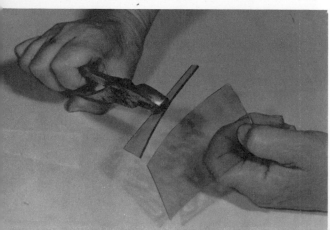

To separate a thin strip of glass from a wider section, grasp the glass on the narrow side of the score line with ordinary pliers or glass pliers and on the other side with your hand. Notice that the glass is always held between the thumb and curled forefinger to provide safe leverage for parting the glass.

To cut out a shaped piece of glass, a different method is employed. Select a pattern templet and lay it on a piece of glass with at least a ¾" margin around the shape. With the fingers of one hand spread out on the templet, hold it firmly against the glass, taking care that it does not slip while you are scoring around it. One side of the glass shape will be scored and separated at a time. Dip the cutter into kerosene and dab it lightly on a paper towel. Begin at one edge of the glass and score along one side of the pattern, continuing beyond it to the opposite edge of the glass *without pausing or lifting the cutter*. Lay down the cutter at once and pick up the glass before the score line heals, as described earlier; applying firm equal pressure on each side of the scored line, snap the glass down and out. If you are cutting off a thin strip of glass, grasp it on the narrow side of the score line with glass pliers or other flat-end pliers and on the other side with the other hand or another pair of pliers. By wrapping narrow masking tape or a thin cloth strip around the pliers's jaws, you can avoid splintering the glass when the hard metal clutches it. It may be necessary to tap sharply along the underside of the score line to *start* the fracture; then press down and out on each side of the fracture line as described for straight cuts. If you try to complete the glass separation by just tapping it until it falls apart, you may have a ragged cut. Cut each side of the shape by scoring and separating it the same way, before you score the next side. When the piece is cut out, remember to sand its edges with fine sandpaper or scrape them with the edge of another piece of glass to remove sharp border slivers. By meticulous attention to this precaution, you can avoid painful cuts.

When you have cut out the curved shape as best you can, you will likely be left with unwanted small projections along its edges. They must be grozed (chipped) away. Although the notches in some glass cutters were meant traditionally to be used for grozing, today many craftsmen prefer to use the jaw tips on a pair of grozing nippers or small pliers to pinch off small projections of glass. If the thickness of the glass fits exactly into one of the notches on the cutter, with care you can chip off irregularities. If the notch is a bit wider than the glass thickness, the projection may take too much glass with it when it separates; you may be left with an unwanted jagged notch instead of an unwanted projection. Because the glass cutting process is fundamentally simple, the novice can pass from nervous frustration to nonchalant skill in a short time. So regardless of how awkward you may feel initially, do not become discouraged.

(Read these instructions over several times until you feel ready and confident to begin the fascinating experience of cutting glass.)

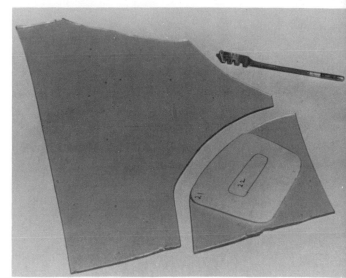

The first cut is made by scoring along one side of the pattern from one edge of the glass to the other.

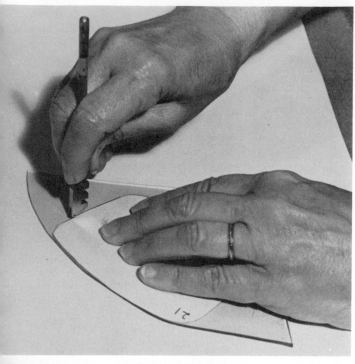

With the fingers of one hand spread out to hold the pattern firmly against the glass, score along the second side from edge to edge of the glass.

A rounded shape is cut out in a series of short curved strokes.

Corners and unwanted projections are "grozed" or nipped off with small flat-nosed pliers or grozing pliers.

A glass storage cabinet. The top section for small pieces is set back to leave shelf space for laying out the small pieces.

Small stained glass free-standing forms. Jack Landis.

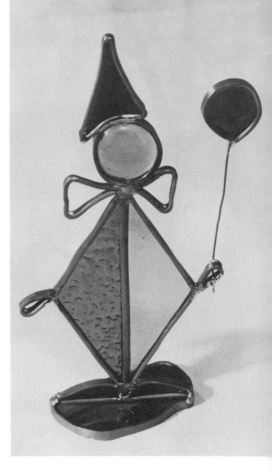

Small stained glass free-standing forms. Jack Landis.

Lead Came

The slender channeled lead stripping that becomes the chief skeletal support in a leaded stained glass construction is called "lead came" (cāme), or just "lead." In addition to holding the glass composition together, lead came becomes a dynamic linear pictorial or abstract design, with the lead lines and colored glass being of equal importance to a successful composition. Structural strength requires that leads run vertically, horizontally, and/or diagonally, not just in parallel lines. Avoid running several lead ends together at one point. What to do with all these ends where they meet would become an aesthetic as well as structural problem. The lead lines are designated first on the original cartoon, then glass colors are selected.

To achieve interest and avoid monotony, lengths and widths of lead should vary. The chief structural lines of the design may be composed of heavier leads than those chosen to delineate delicate details, which can be worked with narrower leads. Important lines should be sweeping and rhythmical with lesser details being more subtle. If you strive to achieve these effects in your preliminary sketches, it will prevent a waste of lead when work is under way.

Lead widths are measured across the top surface rather than across the channeled sides. Lead came is usually available in 6' lengths of various styles and widths. H-shaped lead has double channels with a thin wall or heart between channels. From the end view, this lead is shaped exactly like a capital H, the crossbar in the H representing the thin lead "heart." H cames are used for joining pieces of glass to one another within the composition, and sometimes for border leads where the extra unused outside channel will be puttied or framed into a window. H leads used for the projects in this book are in the range of ⅛" to ¼" wide except for the flat leads used on panel borders, which are wider.

U-shaped lead has one channel and is rounded or flat on the opposite side. It is intended for perimeter leading where a more finished effect is preferred. However, many professionals split a wide H-lead down through the center heart with a chisel and bend the wide strips lengthwise to make their own U leads.

Lead must be stretched and straightened before it can be used. Fasten one end of a lead strip in a vise and pull firmly on the other end with pliers until you feel it stretch. If it is twisted, straighten it and run a pencil or sharpened dowel stick between its flanges to open them. Cut the lead into usable lengths. Use a sharp knife and rock it through the lead gently. (For additional information on using lead, see the section "Leading a Rectangular Panel.")

Rounded and flat H leads have double channels with a thin lead wall between channels. From an end view, the lead is shaped like an H; crossbars represent the lead heart. Glass pieces are fitted into the channels to hold them in a composition.

To stretch lead, fasten one end of a strip in a vise and pull firmly on the other end with pliers until you feel it stretch.

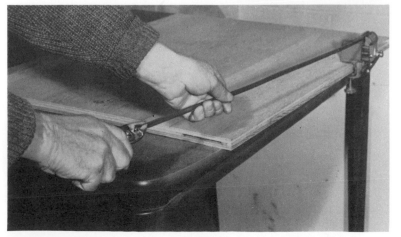

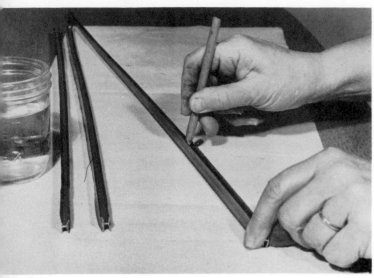

Draw the flattened end of a ¼″ dowel stick along the channels to open them.

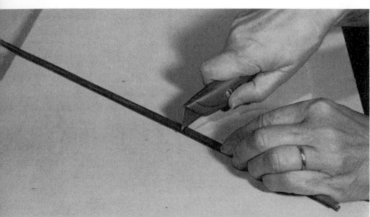

To cut lead, first score it to mark location of the cut, then rock the knife blade gently as you press through the lead.

Soldering

Each separate length of lead came in a stained glass work must be soldered to adjoining pieces of lead. A 100-watt soldering iron with a copper tip and wooden handle heats up readily to workable temperature and is lightweight to hold. The kind of tip you use is a personal choice to some extent and may be limited to whatever is available. Try different size tips if you can, to see how they feel. A small tip is usually preferable for soldering small delicate works or the inside angles of three-dimensional objects such as lanterns and lamps. To avoid the nuisance of unplugging the cord when the iron gets too hot, a simple "on-off" line switch should be installed on the cord about 12 to 14 inches from the handle of the iron. If you want to spend extra money, you may invest in a more professional rheostat control unit. A small stand to rest the hot iron on when it is not in use is imperative.

Before a new soldering iron is used, its copper tip must be "tinned." In this procedure, the first step is to clean it by filing the tip to remove all traces of oxidation and soil. Stroke it smoothly in one direction until it is copper-pink and shiny, taking care to maintain the original planes of the tip. Brush liquid soldering flux over the tip when it has heated. The flux used for all solder work in this book is liquid oleic (ō-lā'-ic) acid. Soldering flux promotes close adhesion between solder and metal; without it the melted solder will roll off in balls. Soldering flux also deters the formation of oxides on the hot metal surface while solder is applied. Over a period of use, some pitting will accumulate on the iron's tip. The tinning process must be repeated from time to time, always starting with a clean filed tip. Solder will not adhere to tarnished or soiled metal. The solder employed both for tinning a soldering iron tip and for joining lead in stained glass work is 60/40 solid core ⅛" wire solder. It contains 60 percent tin and 40 percent lead. (The percentage of tin is always placed first in designating solder.) "Resin core" solders are not suitable for leading stained glass work. They will gum up the glass and lead so much that it will be difficult to clean them.

When the iron's tip has been cleaned and fluxed, plug in the iron and heat it. As soon as solder touched to the tip's surface begins to melt, run the solder all over the planes of the tip to cover it with a thin solder coating. If the solder does not adhere to the tip, the iron is too hot. Cool down the tip to the temperature at which it will accept the solder. Keep the tip clean by brushing it with flux occasionally while you are using it. Avoid inhaling the hot flux fumes.

The melting point of the same 60/40 solid core solder used for tinning the soldering iron tip is just right to use with lead came; the solder melts approximately 10 degrees lower in temperature than lead, which provides an adequate working range. The leads around the juncture area must be cleaned before flux is applied. Brush the lead ends carefully with a copper wire brush or fine sandpaper. When the joints are shiny, dip the solder wire into oleic acid flux and add some to each lead joint with a small brush. To apply solder to the lead, position the tip of the heated iron near the end of the solder wire as it approaches the lead joint and bring them together as they just touch the joint. Use the minimum amount of solder, about ⅛", and press it *lightly* against the joint so the iron rides on top of the solder bead. Hold it there for a second, then lift up the iron before it can melt the lead. It should leave a tiny flat solder puddle. If the solder at the joint "peaks up" too much to suit you, level it by fluxing it again and touching it with the iron tip to flatten it. Practice on scraps of lead before attempting to solder a cherished project. Fill any small gaps between lead joints with little bits of lead before you solder them. Once the first side of your work is soldered, check all junctures carefully to be sure none is missed; then support the panel with one hand beneath it, turn it over, and solder the joints on the other side.

The three most common reasons solder does not adhere to lead are soiled lead, incorrect or insufficient soldering flux, and incorrect soldering iron temperature.

Clean the soldering iron by filing the tip to remove oxidation and soil.

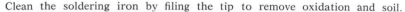

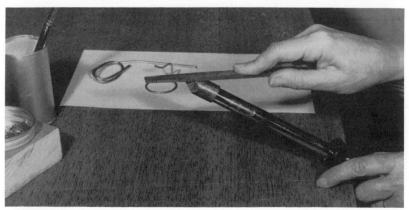

Flux the tip of the iron with oleic acid.

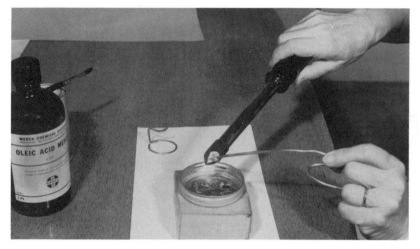

Run solder over the planes of the working tip on the soldering iron; cover it with a thin coating of solder.

It is imperative to rest the hot iron on a special small stand when it is not in use. Otherwise you may burn a tabletop or start a fire.

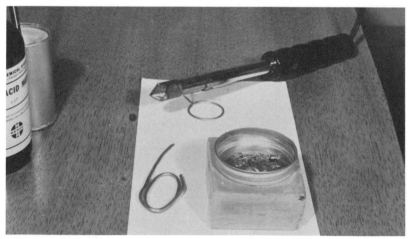

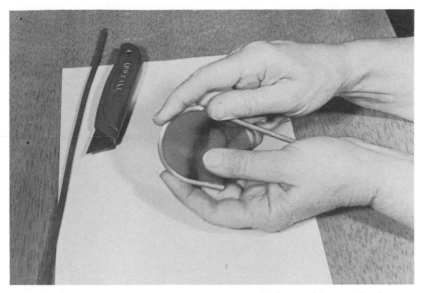

Rounded H leads bend easily around a curved shape without crimping or puckering.

To trim lead ends so they will combine to form a sharp angle, hold the knife blade so it seems to be a continuation of a line that would run through the center of the corner angle. If the end of each corner lead is cut cleanly. you will have a neat juncture for a mitered corner when the lead is fitted to a glass corner or point.

2 * Leaded Stained Glass

A Beginning

IT IS WISE to make a very simple initial stained glass leaded project before you attempt something complex. A four-piece leaded stained glass hanging is easy to make and it requires a minimum of materials. Creating it involves most of the techniques required for fashioning almost any free-form leaded glass object. Design your piece carefully and select glass colors that are compatible and vibrant. Your own simple, successfully executed stained glass hanging will inspire you to create other delightful glass objects to beautify your home; and they make wonderful gifts for all ages.

Before you begin, read carefully the introductory sections on cutting glass, lead came, and soldering. Make a sketch you like and enlarge it to a full-scale drawing (cartoon) divided into three or four sections that are drawn with gently curved or straight lines. Each space represents a piece of colored glass; each line represents a strip of lead. Make two carbon copies of the drawing, one on firm paper that is cut into small patterns for cutting out the glass. A second copy is a work drawing on which you will assemble the project. When the glass pieces are cut, they will be placed on the original drawing nearby to keep them organized and accessible.

Cut out the pattern pieces from the firm paper drawing, using shears to remove a 1/16" paper strip between the sections. The narrow space it leaves will represent the place to be occupied by the heart of the lead. With these small paper templets as guides, cut out glass pieces by following detailed instructions under "Cutting the Glass."

To assemble your hanging, you will need a 3'- or 4' strip of ¼" rounded H lead, a sharp knife for cutting lead, some lath nails, and a hammer. In addition you will need a soldering iron, some 60/40 solid core wire solder, and oleic acid for soldering flux. Tape the work drawing to a workboard and cut a piece of lead long enough to go completely around the glass composition plus a little extra length that can be trimmed later.

The first glass piece is positioned on its matching space in the work drawing. Its outer edge is inserted into the border lead which is positioned so it abuts the drawn borderline of the design along its outside. Lath nails are driven into the workboard (right through the drawing) close against the outside of the lead, and more nails go along the inside bare glass edge to hold the lead and glass securely together while the work proceeds. Cut and fit another lead along one side of the glass with an end trimmed to abut the border lead. Insert the remaining glass pieces into the composition, fitting them with leads that abut the border lead snugly. Lengths of lead fitted between the sides of two glass pieces are always cut about 1/16" shorter than the glass at each end to allow for fitting the remaining glass sides into cross-leads. After each glass is inserted, tap it firmly into the lead with a small wood block held between the glass and the hammer. Never strike the bare glass; you may shatter it. As you continue to bend the border lead around the outside of the assemblage, keep it in place with lath nails. They will all be pulled out when the leads have been soldered.

Once the border lead is in place around the completed composition, trim its two ends for a close fit; butt them together carefully and keep them in place with lath nails. Check to assure that all pieces are tight and lead joints fit flush. Fill any gaps with bits of lead that can be soldered over as you apply solder to each joint. When the first side is soldered (follow directions in the "Soldering" section), remove the lath nails, turn the piece over, and solder joints on the other side.

To make a hanger for your stained glass design, double a 3" or 4" length of 18-gauge copper wire, insert the rounded handle of a small brush into the bent loop end, and twist it three or four times. Spread the free wire ends apart and solder them to the top of your hanging. Now it is ready to be hung wherever moving sunlight will infuse it with shimmering beauty.

Single glass shapes can be leaded as units in a complex construction. Pieces are being soldered together. They are propped on a crumpled pad of paper toweling to hold the construction in place while final pieces are soldered to the assemblage. Complex sculptures are made in this same way.

The completed hanging. Units like these can be strung on wires as mobiles.

Make a full-scale drawing divided into four sections that are drawn with gently curved or straight lines. Trace over it to make two carbon copies.

Antique stained glass lantern. Bette Warner.

Butterfly made of bonded and leaded antique stained glass. Polly Rothenberg.

THREE FACES. Old Dominion Stained Glass Company. Faceted glass set in epoxy. *Courtesy The Blenko Glass Co.*

FLOWERS. Old Dominion Stained Glass Company. Antique stained glass window. *Courtesy The Blenko Glass Co.*

Wind chimes. Fused cathedral glass chimes suspended from weathered wood. Polly Rothenberg.

HOLY FAMILY. Hopcroft Stained Glass Studio. Faceted
glass set in epoxy. *Courtesy The Blenko Glass Co.*

STEMS AND FLOWERS. Polly Rothenberg. Bonded antique
glass. Made for the home of Mr. and Mrs. James Martin.

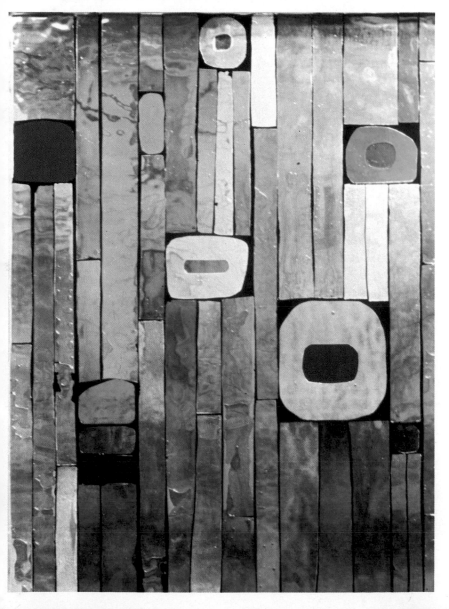

Leaded stained glass hanging.

POTTED PLANT. Bonded and leaded antique glass panel. Polly Rothenberg.

CLOWN. Jack Landis. Free standing figure.

Leaded antique glass fish. Polly Rothenberg.

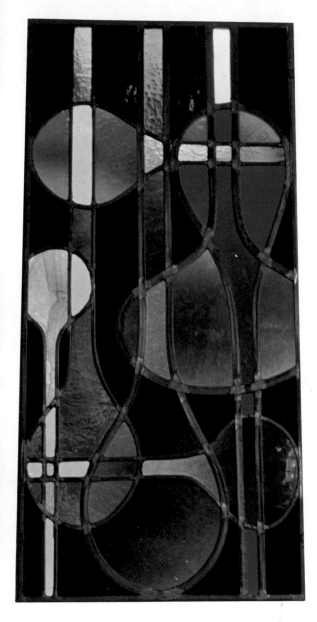

GLASS FORMS. The Franklin Art Glass Studio. Leaded stained glass. *Courtesy The Blenko Glass Co.*

Stained glass door panel. Bette Warner.

Bonded cathedral glass panel. Polly Rothenberg.

MASKS. Jack Landis. Free standing round panel. Painted stained glass.

HOLY FAMILY. Don Shepherd. Cast stained glass sculpture in relief. *Author's Collection.*

CREATION. Laws Stained Glass Studio. Faceted glass set in epoxy. *Courtesy The Blenko Glass Co.*

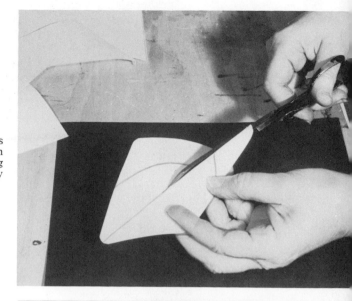

Cut along each side of the *inside* lines to remove a 1/16″ paper strip between sections. The narrow space remaining represents the place to be occupied by the lead heart.

These four sections of firm paper are the patterns around which glass shapes are cut. (See "Cutting the Glass.")

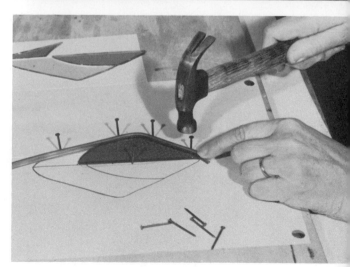

The first glass piece is inserted into the border lead which abuts the drawn border line along the outside of it. Lath nails temporarily hold the glass and lead in place. (Use leading nails if you can find them.)

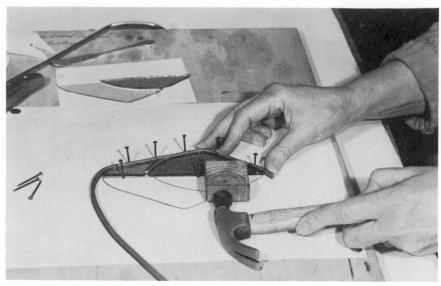

Another lead is cut and fitted along the side of the first glass and a second glass is inserted. Tap the glass firmly into the lead with a small wood block.

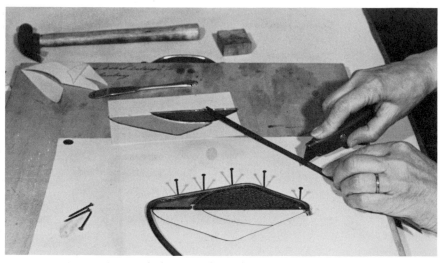

Cut a long lead strip and fit it along the inside edge of the first two glass pieces. To cut the lead, rock the knife gently as you press down. If you press the knife too hard, it will collapse the channels.

Fit lead along a curved edge by holding the glass piece and pressing the lead firmly around the curve.

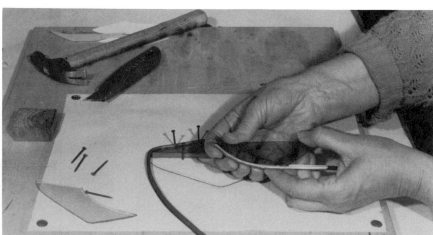

Lengths of lead are always marked and cut a little shorter than the glass to allow for insertion of the glass into cross leads. When the location of the cut has been marked, *remove* the lead to cut it. Trim all lead ends so they abut cross leads snugly parallel.

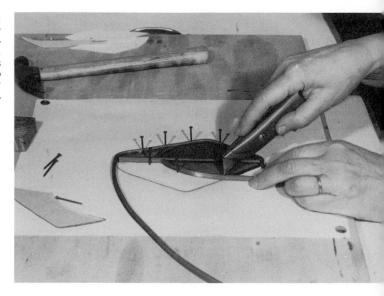

A small gadget for lifting and working a glass piece securely into the lead is made by bending a short butter knife an inch from the end. Support and brace the assemblage with one hand while the other hand works the knife and glass.

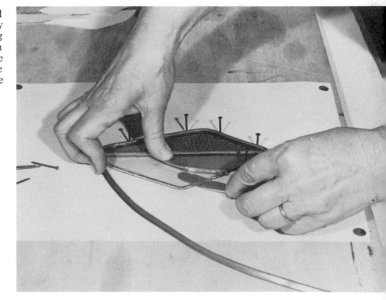

When the last piece is in place, bend the border lead around the completed composition and trim its two ends for a close fit. Hold them securely in place with lath nails.

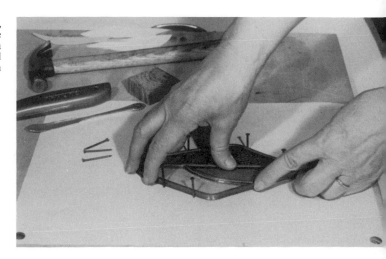

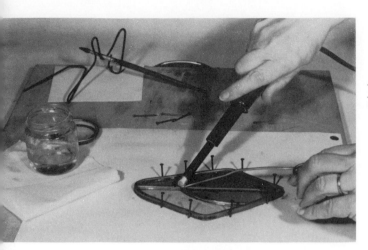

Apply flux and solder to each lead joint, then remove the nails and solder the joints on the reverse side.

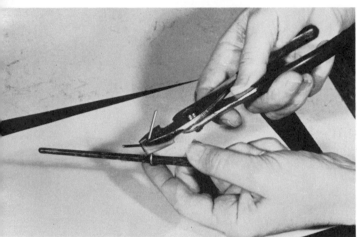

Make a hanger by doubling a 4″ length of copper wire, then twist the loop around a small brush handle.

Clean the wire and lead, then flux them. Anchor the glass hanging in a can of sand or vermiculite to hold it so both hands are free to solder the copper wire in position. Pick up some solder with the hot iron tip and run it over the hanger ends while you press them against the lead. A wooden snap clothespin is convenient for holding the hanger in place.

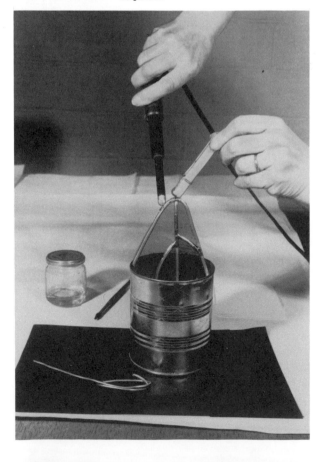

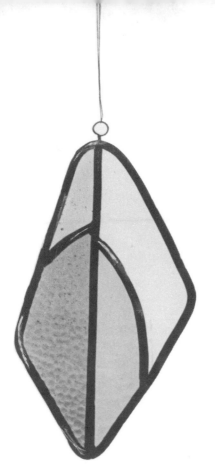

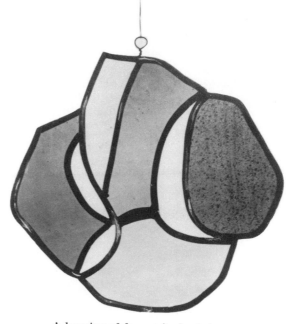

A hanging of four units leaded separately then soldered together with open spaces between them.

The completed hanging.

The Light Table

Although stained glass looks best viewed by natural sunlight, this is not often possible in a studio or home workshop. As you begin to work with a greater number of stained glass shapes a good light table enables you to see relationships of glass colors and their values. It permits you to view several glass colors spread out together. And it is a most important aid for painting on glass. The light table shown here is so simple it can be assembled by anyone if the side and end boards and the legs are precut by a lumber company.

Artificial light rarely approximates natural daylight, but "warm white" fluorescent lights installed at least fifteen inches below a frosted glass top should provide good illumination. The lights are all wired together across the bottom of the table's interior. Wiring runs through the end wall with a single switch installed directly on the outside of the table's end wall. A 10' cord is a wonderful convenience. The table illustrated has ball bearing castors installed on the bottom of each leg. They must be anchored in shallow coasters when the table is in use. Dimensions of this table are: side walls, 30" x 15" x ¾"; end walls, 22½" x 15" x ¾"; legs, 30¼" x 1¾" x 1¾".

Nail the sides and ends together. To brace them securely, the legs are held in place in the corners of the light box with two large C-clamps while bolts are fastened through holes drilled into them and the side and end boards, as shown. The bolts are staggered to avoid interference with one another when they are bolted through the legs to anchor the side and end boards firmly. A space is left at the top of each leg to accommodate ½" strips that will be fastened in place with screws ¼" below the top edge of the table to support ¼" frosted plate glass. A heavy plywood base for the box has its corners cut out so it can be slipped over the legs (the table is upended) and fastened in place with screws. The entire interior of the light box of the table is painted white to give good light reflection and increase illumination. Frosted glass is regular plate glass that can be sandblasted by any large glass company.

Nail the side and end boards of the light table together. To brace them securely, two large C-clamps hold them in position while holes are drilled for bolting the legs to the corner.

A space is left at the top of each leg to leave room for wood strips to support the frosted glass top of the light table.

A plywood bottom for the box is slipped over the legs and fastened in place with screws.

Notice that leg bolts are staggered to allow the leg to be bolted to a side and end board. Lights are being installed across the bottom of the box. The interior is painted white for light reflection.

Patterns and Cartoons

A stained glass window or panel begins with a small-scale drawing that will be transposed into a full-size precise pattern called a "cartoon." Two additional copies of this full-size drawing must be made: a working drawing, and a pattern on heavy paper to be cut into templets. This latter paper must be sturdy but not too thick. Firm drawing paper or light wrapping paper will suffice for the small patterns around which each individual glass piece is cut. Cardboard is too thick; it prevents the glass cutting wheel from riding smoothly around each pattern piece.

The cartoon for a *leaded* stained glass panel must include three important measurements around the border: the *full-size* line, which represents the outside perimeter of the panel's wide flat border lead; the *cut-size* line indicating where the glass pieces next to the border will abut the heart of the border lead; and the *sight-size* line showing the inside edge of the border lead. When the design has been drawn full-scale within these lines, retrace over the lines of the design with charcoal or a felt-tipped marker to make thick lines representing the space to be occupied by the lead heart. It will be the thin lead wall between each glass piece and its contiguous pieces as they are inserted into the stained glass panel. Space allotted to the lead heart must be allowed for in cutting out the pattern pieces and the subsequent matching glass shapes. The next step is to make two copies of the cartoon.

First, lay down the firm paper (from which pattern pieces will be cut); on top of it place a large sheet of good quality carbon paper, carbon side down. If large sheets are not available, butt together several small sheets and tape them on the back with cellophane tape. On top of the carbon paper lay a sheet of paper for the working drawing (to be explained later). Next comes another large sheet of carbon paper. Finally, the precisely drawn cartoon is positioned on top of all. Thumbtack them all securely to the working table or board, pressing each tack firmly through the corners of all these layers to prevent slippage. With a sharp pencil, trace through the *center* of the thick lines of the cartoon carefully and with enough pressure to reach the bottom layer of paper. From time to time as you are tracing, take out one or two thumbtacks to check whether your tracings have gone through all paper layers. Number each space which represents a piece of glass.

When tracing is completed, separate the papers. The *working drawing* will be positioned on the workboard when leading-up begins. The *original cartoon* is located nearby so it can be consulted when necessary. Spaces representing pieces of glass are numbered the same on all three drawings. Colors can be written in pencil, in case of future changes. The *third heavier drawing* will be cut into small patterns representing the glass pieces.

If you have access to a pair of cartoon shears, this is the best tool for cutting out pattern pieces. The shears have a double blade and a single blade. As they cut along the lines of the drawing, a narrow paper strip is removed, leaving a small space between each pattern piece to indicate where the heart of the lead will be positioned between glass

When the design has been drawn full scale between the lines, trace over the lines of the design with a felt-tipped marker.

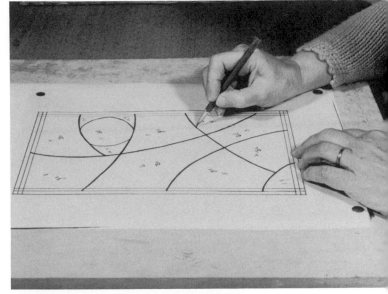

To use the razor blade cutting tool, position the paper pattern on smooth-topped corrugated cardboard which cushions it so the blades can sink through the pattern and cut it.

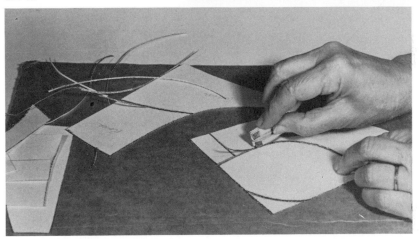

pieces. Cartoon shears are not always available. A substitute device used by beginners can be made by sandwiching a piece of 1/16″ thick cardboard between two single-edged razor blades. They are taped together in two directions. Of course, small sharp scissors can be used to cut along each side of the line to remove it.

To use the razor blade cutting device, position the heavy paper pattern on smooth-topped corrugated cardboard or several sheets of paper to cushion it so the blades of the tool can sink through the pattern and actually cut into it. Draw the blades firmly along so they straddle the pattern lines. Note: the middle or *cut-size* line in the border represents the *edge* of perimeter glass pieces. No narrow paper strip is removed between it and the remaining border area, which is completely cut away with ordinary scissors. If you use the razor blade tool for cutting out pattern pieces, be sure to use new blades or blades that are sharp. When they are pressed firmly and held perpendicular, both razor blades should cut through the paper. You may find that only one blade seems to be cutting completely through the paper, due to a tendency of most persons to hold the tool on a slant; the other blade will at least leave an indented line in the paper that can be cut through with ordinary scissors. If you use the razor blade cutter, press with the corners, not the flat edge of the blades.

Position each cut-out pattern piece on the original cartoon over corresponding numbered spaces. After each paper shape is picked up and a glass shape is cut out around it, both the piece of glass and the paper pattern piece are repositioned on the numbered cartoon. This is the best way to keep all these small shapes organized and easily accessible.

Leading a Rectangular Panel

When all the glass shapes have been cut for a rectangular panel, tape the work drawing to the workbench top if you are planning to complete the panel before you begin another project; otherwise tape it to a workboard that can be moved when necessary. Most plywood is too hard to receive the small nails that will hold your work in place temporarily while you lead it. Cut two ½" thick lath strips, one a little longer than the length of the work drawing and one a little longer than the width. They will guide placement of the lead and glass. Position them at right angles to each other on a lower corner of the work drawing with their *inside* edges abutting the outer *full size* lines of the drawing; this leaves room for the flat border leads. One wood strip runs from top to bottom of the vertical edge of the drawing; the other runs along the horizontal bottom edge of the drawing with one end firmly abutting the vertical wood strip. When both strips are nailed in place (with nails going through the paper drawing), it is time to begin leading up the stained glass.

Lead must always be stretched and its flanges must be opened before it is used. Stretching it straightens out kinks, firms up the lead, and takes up slack in the soft lead so it fits snugly around the pieces of stained glass. If stretching it is neglected, the lead in a stained glass hanging may begin to sag and "let go" the glass at the top where the hanger is fastened, after it has hung for a while. To stretch lead, fasten one end of a lead strip in a strong vise or lead stretcher; grasp the other end with a pair of pliers, and pull it firmly until the lead is taut and its channels are straightened. If it is twisted, untwist it between pulls. When you pull the free lead end with pliers, hold the lead near the pliers with your other hand so you won't fall backward if the lead should break suddenly. Pull firmly until you can feel the lead stretch and become taut. When two persons are working together, each one can pull an end of the lead until it is stretched. Draw the flattened end of a ¼" dowel stick (or a glazier's lathekin) along the channels to open them up so different thicknesses of glass will fit easily between the flanges. If you are using antique glass, you will find that it has varying thicknesses in one sheet of glass, which accounts for its handsome lighter and darker shading of color. When the lead has been stretched, cut it into shorter convenient lengths.

To cut the lead, first score it to mark the location of the cut; then rock the knife blade gently as you press down cautiously through the lead. Too much pressure will collapse the channels. It is wise to practice on scraps of lead. The knife used for leaded projects in this book is a standard matt knife with removable blades that can be replaced or sharpened. They are sold in all art supply stores. If you have access to a glazier's curved knife, of course that is fine, but they are not always available to the novice.

Place the cartoon beside your workboard with glass pieces temporarily in place over corresponding drawn spaces. Give it a final check before leading begins; any changes after this point may waste time and lead. For the border of your panel, cut two stretched and opened lengths of ⅜" flat H head and fit them into the angle of the wooden lath boards you have nailed to the workboard. One lead strip runs along the top of the *lower horizontal lath strip* with its end butting against the *vertical lath strip*. The length of the second lead is pressed against the *vertical lath strip* with its bottom end butting down against the *horizontal lead strip*. (Read these instructions again as you follow them in the illustrations on these pages.) Cut the free ends of the leads longer than is necessary; they will be trimmed when they have been worked into the glass composition. To hold these border leads in place while the first glass pieces are inserted, tack the free ends to the workboard temporarily. Make certain the two leads are butted firmly together in the lower corner. Some craftsmen pinch the lower end of the vertical lead and slip it into the horizontal lead instead of butting it. Either way, avoid leaving gaps between lead joints which will create problems when soldering is under way.

When the two border leads are securely in place, check their flanges to see whether they are still open along their lengths. If they are not, they can be opened with a handy gadget called a "stopping knife," which you can make yourself by bending a short butter knife about an inch from the end. Or saw off part of the blade on a slender table knife. Grind the cut-off end until it is smoothly rounded and bend it about an inch from the end. When the lead channels are clear, press the first glass piece into the channels where they meet at the corner. Make certain the glass is seated securely. Here again, the stopping knife is useful. Slip it under the glass to lift and work it deeper into the corner channels.

The next important step is to place a small block of wood against the glass piece and tap it firmly but gently into the leads. This procedure must be followed after every piece or two are placed, if you would have a snugly fitting firm leaded glass composition. Fit a lead into place along each side of the corner glass piece, butting one end of the lead against the border lead. When you have evaluated how much to cut that end of lead so it will abut at an angle parallel to the border lead for a snug fit, remove it and trim it. Trim the other lead end just a little shorter than the glass to allow for insertion of the glass into the cross lead which divides it from the next row of glass shapes. Build up pieces of glass contiguous to the corner foundation glass shape, fanning out from it and supporting it. As each piece of glass is fitted with lead and inserted into bordering leads, tap it gently with the wood block.

As you build up the glass design, check the drawing under your work to assure that the pieces coincide with the drawn lines. Sometimes a piece will need a minor amount of grozing (chipping) to fit into the space designed for it. But first try tapping it firmly to be sure it is seated and really needs grozing; pieces cut accurately and tapped into the lead securely should need very little trimming. As you work in the glass, avoid surrounding an empty space to the point where a glass shape cannot be inserted into it.

When each piece is fitted with lead and seated, secure it in place *temporarily* with thin, sharp, steel lath nails driven close beside the lead and bare glass sides, two or three nails to a piece. The nails will be pulled out along the working side of each piece as adjoining glass and lead are added. The traditional and useful farrier's (horseshoe) nails used by professional craftsmen are not easy for the novice to locate. They are nonexistent in some localities. The steel lath nails serve our purpose very well; but use the horseshoe nails if you can find them.

Once the glass pieces and leads are all in place, it is time to fit the last two border leads into position. Inspect each glass shape and lead end where it abuts the border. If any glass protrudes over the

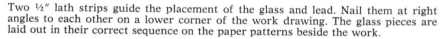

Two ½" lath strips guide the placement of the glass and lead. Nail them at right angles to each other on a lower corner of the work drawing. The glass pieces are laid out in their correct sequence on the paper patterns beside the work.

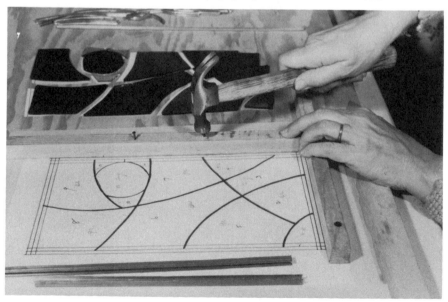

middle (cut-size) line of the border, it should be tapped firmly with the wood block to determine whether looseness in the assemblage is causing the bulge. If there is still some glass extending over the line, remove the piece and groze it for a better fit or replace it with a new piece redesigned to fit. Trim the leads to make a smooth neat border. Finally the flat border leads are positioned over glass and lead ends. Two more lath strips are nailed into position against the border leads to hold them in place. When you have inspected your work and filled any lead juncture gaps with bits of lead, it is time to solder. Do not remove the nails in the lath strips until the first side of the panel is completely soldered. (Read carefully the instructions detailed in the section on "Soldering.")

When both sides of the glass panel have been soldered, push gray glazing compound (putty) against the leads and work it under them with your thumb wherever possible. It holds the glass tight and makes a window weatherproof. Clean up excess putty by running a pointed stick along the leads. Flat border leads are pressed firmly to work out excess compound. Clean away large scraps of glazing putty with your fingers. To absorb and remove the remainder of oleic acid and putty, sprinkle a couple of large handfuls of whiting (calcium carbonate) over the panel and scrub it with a stiff brush. Brush away dust with a soft brush and rags.

Fit two lengths of lead into the angle of the wood lath boards. The first glass pieces will be inserted into the corner of the leads.

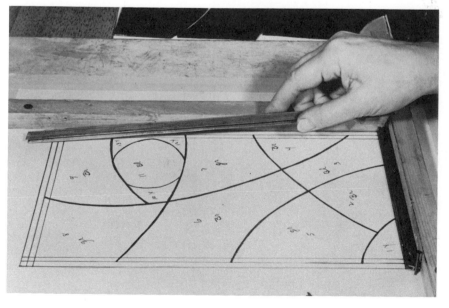

Press the first glass piece into the lead channels where they meet at the corner.

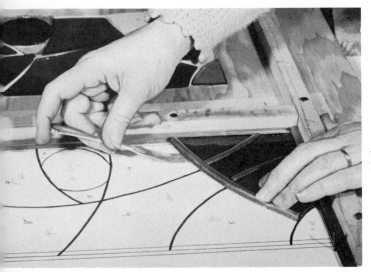

A short bent knife (stopping knife) lifts up the glass to help seat it into the channels of the lead.

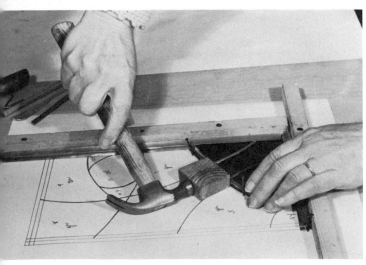

Place a small wood block against the leaded glass and tap it firmly to make a snug-fitting composition.

Small lath nails hold the composition in place temporarily. The leads and glass follow lines in the drawing.

Additional glass pieces and leads are inserted. The bare glass edge borders the middle cut-size line.

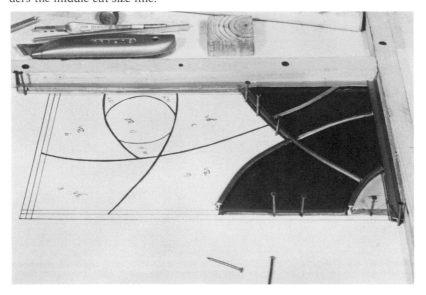

Although a rectangular or square panel is usually leaded up completely before it is soldered, a small grouping of pieces in a larger composition is often soldered into place to hold it secure as the panel is assembled.

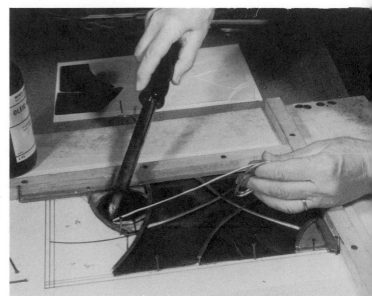

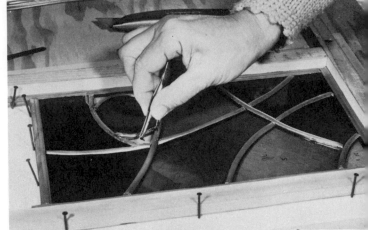

All glass and leads are in place; final border leads are positioned and anchored with nails and a third lath strip. Fill any gaps in the lead junctures with bits of lead, then solder all the joints.

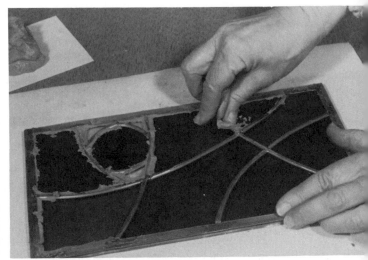

Push gray glazing compound (putty) against and under each lead with your thumb. It holds the glass tight and will make a window panel weatherproof.

Remove excess putty by running a pointed dowel stick, meat skewer, or pencil along all the leads.

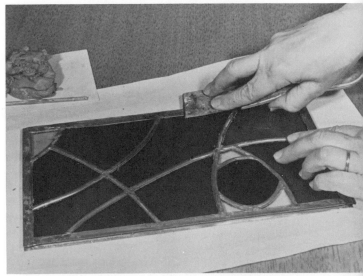

Flat border leads are pressed smooth with a putty knife to work out excess compound.

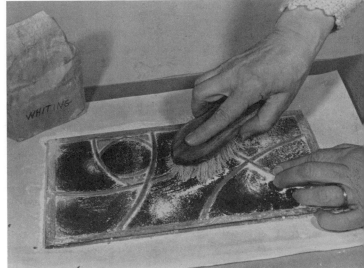

Clean away scraps of glazing compound and oleic acid by sprinkling several handfuls of whiting (calcium carbonate) over the panel and scrub it diligently with a stiff brush. Brush away remaining crumbs with a soft brush and a rag. The panel can be hung; or you can make three additional panels to combine into a lantern as shown on the following pages.

A Four-Panel Lantern

Lanterns formed with four rectangular panels are handsome, practical, and simple to make. Begin by making the panels complete, following precisely the instructions given in the preceding sections. The designs may be similar for all four panels, or they may alternate. Keep them simple and use medium- and light-density glass colors. To prevent the light fixture from showing, the top should be formed of metal or opalescent glass. A top made from glass sections is not the easiest kind to make for an initial project. The top for the demonstration lantern is an upside-down copper tray, the kind found in metal-enameling supply shops or in metal supply catalogs. You will be delighted to discover a variety of lovely copper trays of many sizes and shapes—square, round, octagonal, and the like—that can become wonderful lantern tops. A ⅜″ hole must be cut in the metal top to accommodate electric wiring and a top ring for holding the chain or rope hanger. If you are not able to cut the hole, any metalwork shop will do it for a nominal amount of money.

Panel dimensions for the demonstration lantern are 6½″ by 11″. Border leads are ⅜″ flat H leads; leads for the panel design are ¼″ with the exception of the rounded glass piece which is fitted with ⅛″ lead. On each panel side edge, the border lead flange which faces toward the *inside* of the lantern is bent to about a 90° angle to the panel, permitting the *outside* flanges at each corner to butt together. Stand the first two panels on end at right angles to each other, as illustrated in the accompanying photograph. Prop them in place with any straight-edged blocks such as bricks. Pinch the bent lead flanges together down the inside of the corner and solder them along the edge. A small soldering-iron tip is most convenient for the inside corners.

Set the third panel in position and support it with additional bricks. Once it is soldered in place, lay the assemblage down with the remaining open side toward the tabletop. Support the two panels that rest on the table with bricks laid against their outside surfaces while the fourth panel is positioned between them and soldered, first from one end, then from the other. The demonstration lantern is set upside down so 8-gauge copper wire that has been annealed can be soldered into the bottom lead channels all around the four sides, to reinforce them. A small bit of the lead heart in the lower end of each vertical corner lead must be cut out so the wire can pass through the bottom lead channels and *around corners*. Anneal the wire by heating it red hot, then dousing it in water. Annealing metal makes it pliable and easy to work. Until the square top is soldered to the lantern, care must be exercised in handling it to keep the four joined panels in a right-angled position. Once the firm metal top is in place, it will keep the lantern squared. The copper tray top is 7½″ square.

If you want to conceal the juncture crack between the leads that run down the length of each outside corner of the lantern, split some ⅜″ or ½″ H leads down through the heart with a chisel or shears to make flat lead strips. Tack a strip to each corner with solder, top and bottom. Press the soft lead smoothly against and around each corner with your fingers and solder it in several additional places along the edges. Set the completed body of the lantern aside while the square copper top (with a ⅜″ hole cut in it) is scrubbed clean with scouring powder, rinsed, dried, and set upside down on a bench wheel.

The solder used for bonding the copper top to the lantern is 40/60 low-fusing self-fluxing paste solder called "Fast." This type of solder is doubtless available under other trade names. Copper oxidizes so quickly when heat is applied that the 60/40 solid core wire solder used for leading cannot be used for bonding copper to lead. An exception is the instance of soldering copper wire (which heats up rapidly) for hangers to suspend stained glass objects. Self-fluxing paste solder excludes air from the metal surface, which prevents oxidation and allows bonding readily. Set the lantern upside down on the copper top and mark its intended location with a pencil. Remove the lantern and brush paste solder along each section of the copper top, over the pencil marking.

Set the lantern upside down again on the metal top, carefully matching the lantern to the brushed solder. There are bound to be a few crevices between the lantern leads and the metal top. Cut some small flat slivers of lead and brush solder on both surfaces of the lead pieces. Insert two or three of them securely against the juncture between the metal top and the lantern on each side. Once all the lead bits are in place, it is time to apply heat. Since low temperature will melt this solder, a propane cylinder torch, the kind bought in hardware stores, works very well. Hold some asbestos paper in front of the lantern's glass and lead to protect it while you apply heat from beneath the copper top, as illustrated. Hold the flame directly beneath the soldered area and play it back and forth slowly. Keep close watch over it. As soon as the solder turns silver and shiny, *remove the torch.* Leave the lantern undisturbed for a few minutes before you set it upright, to be sure the solder has hardened.

Most large electric lamp and fixture stores carry an assortment of accessories for lanterns. The parts employed in the lantern shown here are a lamp ring (also called a loop), a threaded nipple, a light socket, and a separator plate that fits between the metal lantern top and the threaded nipple. The lantern is hung with a decorative chain.

Stand the first two panels on end at a right angle. Prop them securely in place with any straightedged blocks such as bricks. Solder them together along the inside of the corner angle.

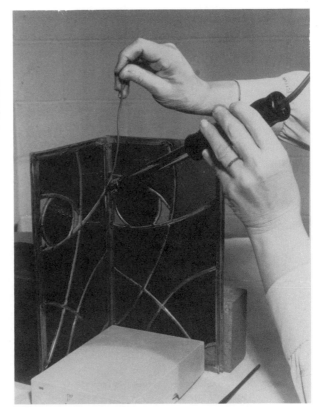

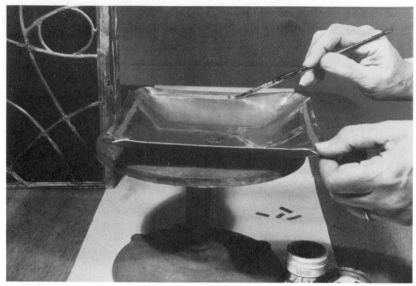

Brush low fusing 40/60 paste solder along each section of the copper top where the lantern will be positioned. Notice the small lead pieces that will be soldered into the juncture between the lantern and its top.

Hold asbestos in front of the glass and lead to protect them from the torch as you play it slowly along under the solder.

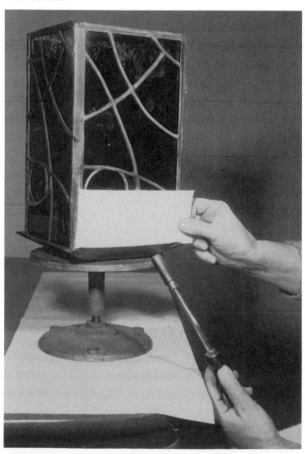

The completed lantern with electric fittings. Antique stained glass provides undulating charm.

A Free-Form Leaded Panel

There are two chief differences between leading the free-form panel and leading a straightedged shape. First—the leads in the free-form design sometimes extend outward and become part of the border leading; there is no continuous framing lead. For this reason ¼″ H lead is used throughout the illustrated free-form composition. The second chief difference—lead junctures are soldered as your work progresses. Instead of leading from a corner and working out in a fan-shape direction, apply and solder the leads straight across the panel composition, beginning at any point on the panel perimeter. In the demonstrated design, the center glass piece, number 8, is also leaded as part of the first row of work. Otherwise, the space for it would be encircled by the border pieces and the center glass could not be worked into its designated position. Be sure to tap the glass into the leading with a wood block as you work. If a glass piece does not fit correctly, replace it. One glass piece bulging over its encircling lines will prevent contiguous pieces from fitting into their appointed positions.

Small leaf shapes along the outer edge of the design have well-defined corners. To maintain this crisp effect, the lead is cut apart at each corner and the ends are mitered together again. Cut the lead ends so the *juncture* appears to continue on a line with the point of the glass corner. You may have to use separate leads instead of cutting one lead apart to achieve the sharp point. When each glass has been tapped into place with the wood block, anchor it with lath nails along the working edge while you solder the lead juncture. Then remove the nails and fit another glass with lead, and so on until the project is complete. Remove the nails from around the panel. Glazing a hanging is optional, but many persons do glaze hangings to give them a firm finished quality. To complete the project, solder a wire hanger to the top as described under "A Beginning."

A freeform shape in leaded glass. Bright blue, green, and red. The body of the fish is leaded first, then tail and fins, beginning with the rear fins. Open spaces are left between the rear fins and the body.

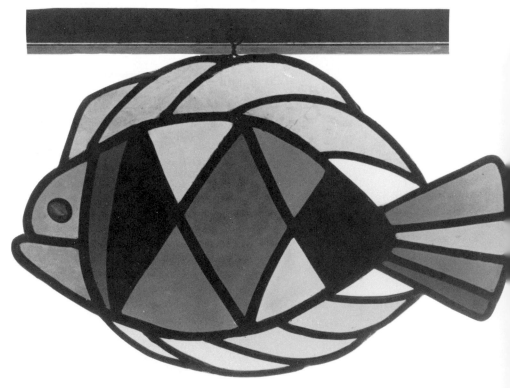

Glass shapes are laid out on the light table to check colors and values.

The interior leads in this freeform design extend outward to become part of the border glass lead, then they curve into the interior again. There is no continuous framing lead.

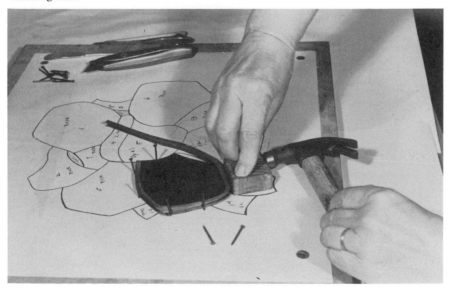

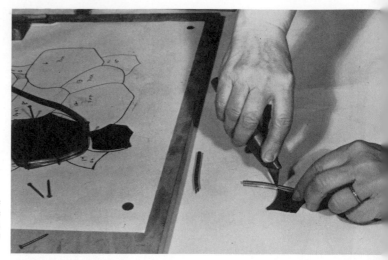

Small leaf shapes have well defined corners. The lead is cut apart at each corner and the ends are mitered together again.

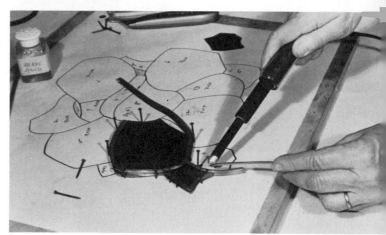

Lead joints in a freeform design are soldered as the leading progresses.

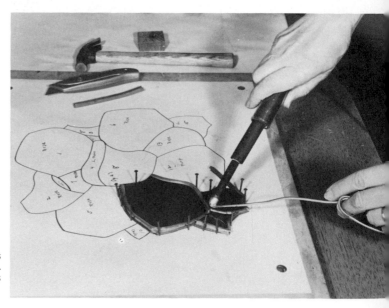

Apply and solder the leads straight across the panel. Include the center glass piece with the first row.

As you work, anchor the leads all around the edge of the assemblage with lath nails until the project is complete, then remove the nails.

A colorful antique glass panel makes a decorative and striking window treatment against the sun or snow. Colors are rose, amethyst, olive, and green. The center and one leaf are opalescent in rose and green.

3 * Glass Bonded
with Epoxy Resin

SMALL STAINED glass shapes are epoxied to a larger sheet of clear colorless glass to make attractive bonded panels or windows. A bonded glass composition does not have the supportive linear quality of leaded glass. Without some variation provided by dark glass colors, the design will appear weak unless, of course, strong lines are provided by dark grouting applied between glass shapes. The clear glass base used in these demonstration projects is double-strength window glass.

The undulating quality that gives beauty to antique glass makes it difficult to bond without causing large irregular bubbles to form between it and the clear glass base. If you do not care for this effect, it is suggested that you use rolled cathedral glass which has one smooth surface, suitable for bubble-free bonding. The glass must be prepared *before* the epoxy is mixed. For safety's sake, all glass edges are sanded smooth. The stained glass and the clear glass base are washed with hot detergent water, rinsed in warm water, and dried completely. Take care to hold the glass by its edges to avoid transferring skin oil to the clean surfaces. Epoxy will not bond securely to damp or soiled glass.

Epoxy adhesives come in two containers, one the resin and the other the hardener. The two components must be blended thoroughly before use. For very small projects, epoxy can be bought in tubes. Epoxy resin is usually bought in quarts or gallons for large or important projects.

50

It is important to use *epoxy* resin and hardener especially formulated for glass on glass bonding.* *Polyester* resins usually shrink
when they dry and they may set up stresses in the glass which can
cause large bonded glass projects to crack. Before epoxying begins,
clear the tabletop and the surrounding area where the work will be
done. The tabletop *must be level* so pieces do not slide out of position
while the adhesive is drying. Mix only the amount you can apply in
20 to 30 minutes. Work diligently so all pieces are epoxied and pressed
into place before the adhesive starts to set. The resin, the hardener,
the glass pieces, and the workroom temperatures should be kept
between 75° and 85°F throughout the process. Be sure the area is well
ventilated and avoid inhaling the fumes. Wear thin plastic gloves which
can be bought in paint stores. Some skins are sensitive to resins. If
you follow the manufacturer's directions explicitly, you will have a
successful bonding.

A thin film of epoxy provides the greatest adhesive strength when
sheet glass is bonded. Epoxy has a different rate of expansion from
that of glass. When stained glass is bonded to plate glass or double-
strength window glass in large windows or panels, stresses may be
set up in the glass if the panel is exposed to bright sunlight for long
periods of time. Stained glass absorbs heat faster than clear colorless
glass and tends to expand imperceptibly; the darker the glass, the
greater the strain. Pieces of stained glass encased completely in resin,
above and beneath it, are likely to crack when the stained glass begins
to expand. But a thin layer of epoxy under the glass pieces causes
less strain and less hazard of breakage if the pieces are less than 8"
long. When a design calls for a long piece of dark glass, it is wise to
use a series of shorter pieces with 1/16" spaces between segments.

Many beautiful and successful works in bonded stained glass
have been achieved by careful adherence to adequate preparation of
the glass and correct application and kind of epoxy adhesive.

Bonding Glass—Random Shapes

Odd-shaped glass remnants obtained from a glass studio or an
art glass supply company often make interesting and beautiful compositions when they are bonded to ordinary window glass with epoxy
resin. Because studio glass scraps were separated from actual glass
designs, many of them have exciting and useful shapes. For your first
project, it may be best to select the light colorful hues until you
become familiar with the best way to include dark shades as accents
in a composition.

Lay a sheet of double-strength window glass on the light box or
on white paper so the glass colors are easily seen. Spread a number
of glass pieces directly on the window glass and move them around
until you have a pleasing arrangement. They may be laid closely
together or with spaces between them. Some pieces may require minor
trimming or grozing (see "Cutting the Glass"). When you have made
a final selection of stained glass shapes, wash, rinse, and dry the glass
as described earlier. The clean colored glass pieces are positioned on

---

* Epoxy used for *sheet glass* bonding projects in this book is Thermoset
Resin #600 with Thermoset Hardener #37.

clean paper to one side of the window glass in the relationship they will have on this clear pane of glass when they are bonded. It is helpful to make a full-size drawing of the final arrangement of pieces and put it under the window glass to guide placement of the epoxied stained glass shapes.

Read carefully all directions on the epoxy containers before you mix resin and hardener as specified. Blend the two parts thoroughly. As you apply the adhesive in a thin coat to the underside of each glass shape, press it firmly in place on the pane of clear glass. A spreading stick can be wiped clean with a rag or paper towel that is discarded at little cost. Should you apply epoxy with a brush, in a short time your brush will accumulate a mass of resin in various stages of hardening and it may have to be discarded. When all glass pieces are in place, let the panel dry on the table for at least 24 hours. If any pieces are moved after the epoxy starts to set, partially set resin will show up as cloudy distortions through the glass.

When the epoxy is completely set, grout may be applied between the stained glass shapes. Mix powdered grout with water to damp clay consistency. Pack it between glass shapes with the edge of a tiny spatula or cardboard, then smooth it evenly. Remove all surplus grout from the tops of glass pieces immediately; it will be difficult to remove after it sets. To keep grout from cracking while it dries, cover the panel closely with plastic sheeting for eight hours. White grout can be painted with India ink when it is dry. Grouting for projects in this book is ceramic tile grout bought in commercial tile stores. Companies that make this grout make coloring material to blend with the dry grout before it is mixed with water.

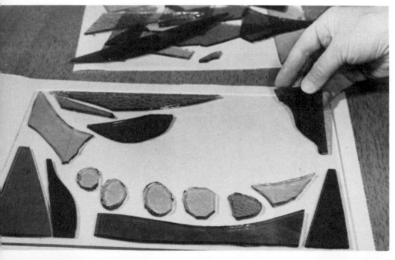

Spread random stained glass pieces directly on the clear glass sheet and move them around until you have a pleasing arrangement.

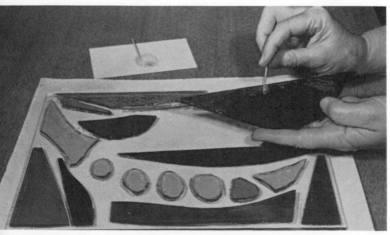

Apply epoxy in a thin even coat to the underside of each glass piece and press it firmly in place.

As soon as grout is packed into all spaces between the glass, immediately remove all excess grout from the glass with water and a sponge before the grout dries. It is difficult to remove after it has set.

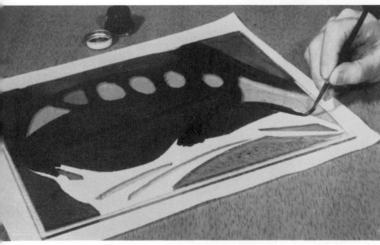

The white grout can be painted with two coats of India ink; or grout can be mixed with grout color before it is used.

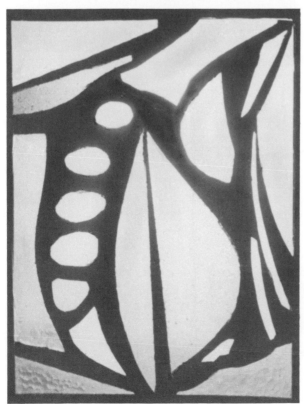

Black grout and glass make contrasting patterns.

Bonding Glass—Designed and Cut Shapes

Three identical drawings are made for a designed bonding project in the same way the drawings are prepared for a leaded glass project, with the exception that only one border line is made on each drawing. This line indicates the outer limit of applied stained glass shapes. *One drawing* is cut into small patterns representing glass pieces. The glass shapes are cut out around the patterns, carefully washed and dried, and arranged in their correct sequence on the *cartoon*. The *work drawing* is taped to the workboard, and a sheet of clean, double-strength window glass is positioned on top of it so extra drawing paper extends beyond the glass. The window glass should be the exact size of the drawing *plus a margin of ¼″* all around to allow for mounting the finished panel. Tape the glass sheet securely to the drawing with the masking tape extending over this ¼″ margin all around the glass edge. No stained glass or epoxy will be applied to this margin. Putty or thin wood strips will cover the margin when the completed panel is installed or framed. The masking tape must be *removed* when the epoxy begins to set and become rubbery, but *before it hardens*. Otherwise the epoxy will seal it firmly to the glass.

A heavy cardboard or plastic container, plastic measuring spoons, two plastic ¼-cup measures, a small scale such as a postage scale, stirring sticks, spreaders, and a can of epoxy solvent that should be bought at the time the resin is purchased are placed on a nearby table or shelf. These supplies should fill requirements for bonding a simple panel. Clean rags or paper toweling will be needed to clean up after epoxying is completed.

When everything is ready, don your gloves and prepare to mix the epoxy. Remember—the success of your bonded project depends on *following exactly* the manufacturer's instructions. Mixing directions vary for different resin-hardener combinations. Thermoset Resin #600 and Thermoset Hardener #37 were used for these bonding projects. The resin becomes cloudy when it is first mixed with hardener due to tiny bubbles formed through chemical action. The two components must be blended very thoroughly. About twenty minutes after they have been mixed, the cloudiness begins to disperse and the epoxy is applied. As it dries, it becomes clear. OTHER RESINS MAY MIX DIFFERENTLY. Do not mix up more epoxy than you can apply in 20 to 30 minutes. A half ounce of resin and of hardener makes a considerable amount. The beginning tends to mix too great a quantity at one time.

Once the ingredients have been blended for the required amount of time (consult manufacturer's directions), pick up a clean piece of stained glass, spread it thinly and evenly with epoxy, position it exactly, and press it firmly in place on the clear sheet of glass, following the drawn design underneath the window glass. Continue epoxying and applying glass pieces and pressing firmly. If you plan to apply grout between glass shapes when the epoxy has dried, the resin that oozes out between glass pieces when you press them down must be removed with a toothpick or other means and wiped on paper toweling. If the epoxy is left to fill the cracks, there will be no place for the grout. By this time you may have smeared some epoxy on the pieces of stained glass. Do not be too concerned; as soon as the epoxy has started to set and become rubbery, but *before it hardens*, it can be scraped away with a razor blade and removed completely with epoxy solvent. Always wear plastic gloves when you use solvents; if this is neglected the solvent may carry chemicals deep into your skin. Use the very minimum amount of solvent.

Check the epoxied stained glass pieces from time to time to make certain they have not shifted. As long as they move quite easily, they can be slid gently back into place. If some pieces touch one another or are farther apart than others, it will add a pleasing casual effect, typical of bonded glass work. *Do not move* the glass shapes once the epoxy begins to set. When all glass pieces are pressed into place, leave the panel undisturbed (except for cleaning up) for a minimum of 24 hours. The bonding achieves its greatest strength after seven days.

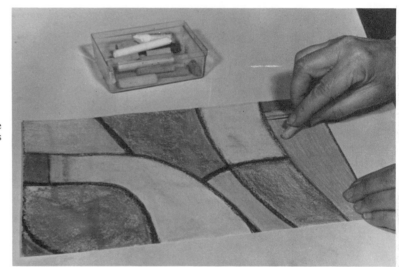

A design is drawn full scale in color for a bonded glass panel.

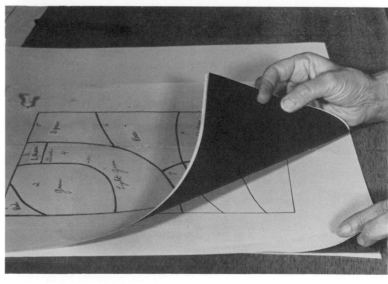

Three identical drawings are made of the panel design.

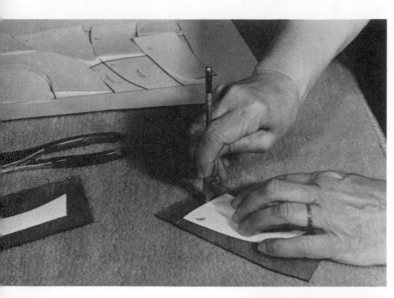

One drawing is cut into small patterns. Glass shapes are cut out around the small patterns, one side at a time.

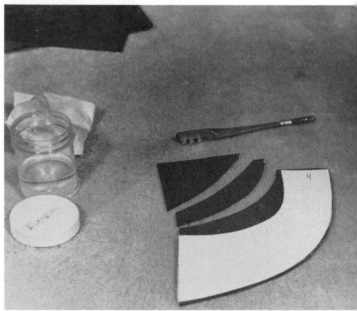

Deep curves are cut in shallow sections, one at a time.

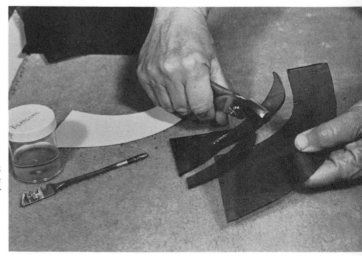

The narrow piece of glass is separated with pliers while one hand bends the larger section outward.

Each cut piece of glass is positioned on the cartoon along with its pattern piece, to keep all these small shapes organized and convenient.

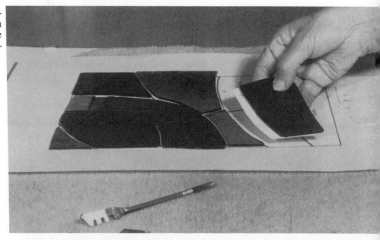

A final check of all shapes and colors is made over the light table.

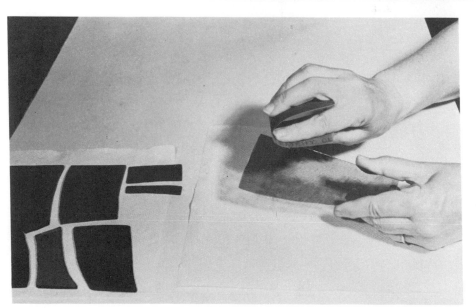

Sand the edges of newly cut glass to remove thin sharp slivers that appear along new cuts.

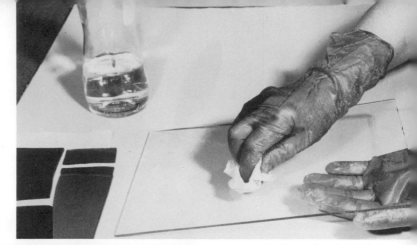

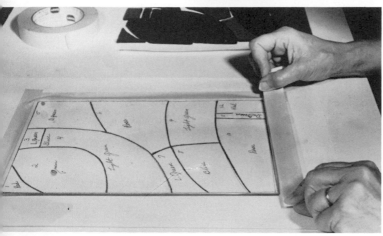

The glass is cleaned and dried. It is wise to wear gloves whenever you work with chemicals.

Tape the work drawing to the workboard. Tape the glass sheet securely to the drawing with masking tape extending over a ¼" margin all around the glass edge.

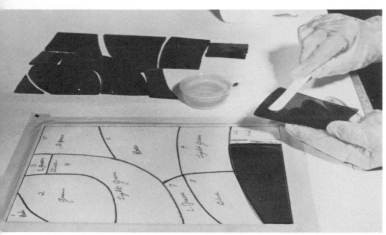

Spread epoxy thin and even over each glass shape and press it firmly in place on the clear glass sheet following the drawn design under the glass.

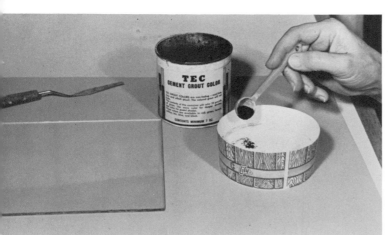

Dry black grout colorant is mixed with white grout before water is added.

Mix the grout, the colorant and enough water to make stiff paste consistency. Blend it with a paint spatula for several minutes until it is smooth.

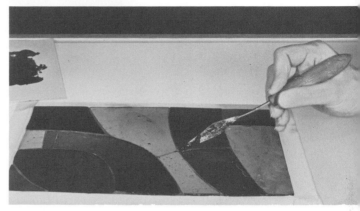

Work the grout into each crevice until it is even with the glass surface. Clean off the surplus grout immediately before it dries.

Undulating antique glass panels are decorative and cheery in any window. Colors are rose, blue, olive green, and red.

Bonding Faceted Glass *(Dalles-de-Verre)* *

The imaginative use of slab glass segments is rapidly forming a major new glass craft in this country and in Europe. It is reminiscent of an old craft practiced by the Egyptians and the Byzantines when thick glass was the only kind available to them for creating windows and mosaics. Faceted slab glass is an antique variety cast into thick slabs that are generally 8" × 12" or 12" × 12", having a thickness of ½" to 1"; it is cut or chipped to give it sparkling facets. Segments of the glass are sometimes bonded into panels with cement; but weather peculiarities make cement-bonded glass impractical for exterior use in cold or variable climates. Today, professional craftsmen are bonding faceted glass with a special adhesive sometimes mixed with sand. The epoxy used for the demonstration project is Thermoset #116 Epoxy and Hardener, which is available in several appropriate colors. This two-component adhesive has been formulated specifically to give structural strength, durability, and weather resistance to interior or exterior slab glass installations.

Before the project begins, all glass pieces are washed in hot detergent water, rinsed in warm water, and dried. Boards are nailed together to make a frame of correct dimensions into which the panel is cast. When the frame has been lacquered and dried, seal the inside of the corners with masking tape. Wax the inside of the frame with plenty of hard paste wax. Set it aside and prepare the base of the frame.

A full-size drawing showing the position of the glass in the panel is laid out on a ¾" thick sheet of plywood and covered with a transparent parting sheet such as polyethylene sheet, fiber glass laminate, or other plastic. Anchor the wood frame in position over it by nailing small blocks of wood against the outside of the frame with the nails going into the plywood through the parting sheet and the paper, which extend beyond the frame. Toe a few nails into the frame and the plywood. The parting sheet is also given a coat of the hard paste wax.

The bottom sides of the glass segments must be sealed off to prevent epoxy from running under them. A material such as latex (Thermoset 529 was used for the demonstration project) is both a sealant for the glass and a release agent for the parting sheet and the frame when the epoxy has matured. Brush some latex on the inside of the frame and paint the bottom of each glass with latex before setting it inside the frame in its designated position. When all the glass is in place on the parting sheet, pour a thin layer of latex, *no thicker* than ⅛", over the parting sheet between glass pieces. Keep the glass clean and wear gloves if you touch it. After about 24 hours, if the latex is dry, it is time to prepare the epoxy resin and hardener. If any glass piece is deeply faceted around its top edge, fill in the facets with putty to shield them from the epoxy. It can be dug out later.

Resin is always supplied with hardener as a unit. They must be mixed together thoroughly. If you have access to a paint shaking mixer, it is a good blending device. Shake it for five minutes; but remember, the epoxy begins to activate as soon as it is blended! If

* Information by courtesy of Thermoset Plastics, Incorporated, Indianapolis, Indiana.

less than the entire amount in a container will be mixed, the resin and hardener must be weighed out in exactly the same proportions specified in the manufacturer's instructions. The pouring table must be level. The epoxy eventually levels out completely, so take care you do not pour so much that it runs over the shorter glass pieces. As soon as the epoxy is blended, it is poured between the glass to a height no greater than ⅝". To provide a sanded surface, sift the sand over the epoxy about 15 to 20 minutes after the casting.

The resin and hardener for the demonstration project, charcoal gray Thermoset #116 Resin and Hardener, was hand mixed with a stout stick for five minutes. It was continually scraped down the sides and *stirred from the bottom up*, which brought up very thick material including dark sand. When the thick material is stirred, you may have some misgivings at first about being able to pour it. But do not be concerned; when the thin hardener is added to it and completely blended for five minutes, it acquires a wonderful texture and pourable viscosity that will make you marvel at the manufacturer's skill. Be sure to stir it from the bottom, and do not mix it longer than five minutes or it may begin to heat up and may set too soon.

Afer considering several kinds of pouring vessels to find one that could be manipulated easily, a half-gallon milk carton was selected. It was filled half full for each pouring, then refilled again. By squeezing a corner slightly for a pouring spout, a thin stream of the mix can be controlled and poured into narrow spaces between the glass pieces. Because an entire gallon container of epoxy was mixed, in order to use up the surplus epoxy an extra smaller round panel was prepared at the time the rectangular demonstration project was made; heavy linoleum was substituted for the wood frame. A piece of copper pipe ⅞" wide and ¾" long was set into the latex release agent ½" from the edge of the linoleum frame at the time the glass was positioned to provide a hanging device for the panel.

Panels cast with this epoxy compound should cure for 24 hours at normal room temperature. After that time the latex sealant is stripped from it. Allow three to four days before installation.

A full-size drawing is laid out on a sheet of plywood and covered with a transparent parting sheet. The wood frame is anchored over it. Frame and base are given a coat of hard paste wax.

Liquid latex brushed over the inside of the wood frame provides a release agent for the epoxy panel.

The bottom of each glass is coated with latex before it is set in place. The latex turns translucent and light tan as it dries.

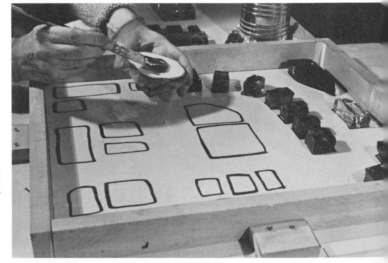

When all glass is positioned, the thin latex is poured over the parting sheet between glass pieces. It should not be poured over ⅛" thick.

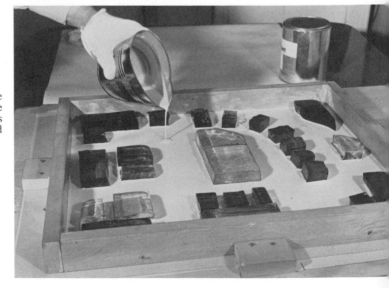

A half-gallon milk carton makes an excellent pouring vessel for the heavy dark epoxy that is poured over the dry latex. Notice the linoleum frame in the background into which excess epoxy will be poured for a smaller panel.

By squeezing a corner of the carton for a pouring spout, a thin stream of the mix is poured into narrow spaces.

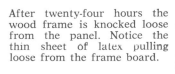

After twenty-four hours the wood frame is knocked loose from the panel. Notice the thin sheet of latex pulling loose from the frame board.

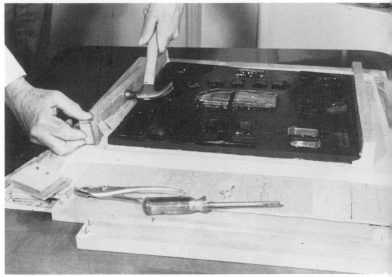

The latex release sheet is stripped easily from the panel.

The completed panel.

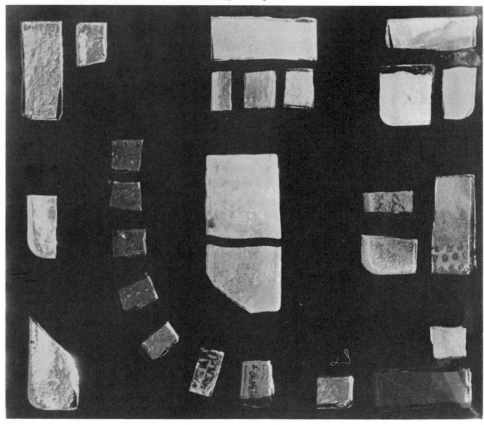

4 * Other Stained Glass Forms

Painting on Glass—Fired

ALTHOUGH THE lavish painting of stained glass cathedral windows during the final stages of the Renaissance period cast the art into controversy for many decades, today the restrained and thoughtful use of fired paints can add decorative variation to plain colored stained glass. Chief supplies for simple glass painting are special brushes, a glass palette, a spatula for mixing and blending the paint, and small pointed tools for carving dried paint. Regular glass paint is required. Glass painting on large professional projects is much more complex than the simple process described here.

Paints used for the demonstration projects are Thomas C. Thompson's Glass Decorating Colors. There are excellent paints made by other companies especially for use on glass. Glass paints should fire smooth and shiny at about 1120°F (or cone 022), well below the temperature at which glass softens. The dry powdered paints can be mixed with water or a light oil such as lavender oil or squeegee oil. Oils dry more slowly than water, and they promote a smooth flowing application of paint; the oil does not leave an ash.

China painting liner brushes (pure red sable) are ideal for fine, long, smooth lines and details. The brush used for projects in this book is a #4 red sable liner. Its bristles are long, thin, and flexible.

Prepare the glass by cleaning it with alcohol, acetone, or thin detergent water. Rinse away the cleaning film with plenty of warm water and dry the glass thoroughly. Tape the glass over a design

65

drawn on a paper which extends beyond the glass piece. The glass and pattern can be rotated on the light box as work progresses. You can apply your strokes in the direction easiest for you to control just by turning the paper. An armrest or "bridge," made from a board with flat wood blocks nailed under each end, will elevate your hand and wrist above the glass surface while you work. It will prevent them from smearing the paint or soiling the glass with oil from your skin. Make the bridge long enough so that the blocks rest on the frame of the light box, not on its glass top.

Prepare the dry powdered paint by placing a small mound of it on the glass palette and adding drops of squeegee oil or other medium as you mix and blend it with a small paint spatula. Work it into a free-flowing homogenous mass of good brushing consistency. To load the brush, roll it in the paint and work plenty of pigment into the bristles; then stroke the brush once or twice on the bare glass palette to relieve it of excess paint. It must retain enough paint to flow nicely through a complete stroke without suddenly going dry. The most beautiful strokes are those that swing easily into a freehand approach. This method takes experience and practice. Make the strokes the best way you can; then let the paint dry before you carve away irregularities with a pointed round toothpick, a sliver of pointed bamboo, or some other scriber.

If you are firing one glass piece, set it on a prepared section of insulation brick that has been rubbed with dry whiting for a separator, then sifted with kiln wash. If you are firing several pieces of glass, coat a clean kiln shelf with whiting rubbed in with the fingers, sifted, or mixed with water to thin cream consistency and applied with a brush, then sift it with kiln wash. If the latter method is used, paint the shelf with water before applying whiting; the wet shelf must dry overnight or longer. When the insulation brick or shelf has been prepared, put the glass into a cool kiln before you turn it on. If the kiln is a front loader, position the glass well toward the rear of the kiln; if it is a top loader, keep the glass away from kiln walls.

With the glass in place, turn the heat to *low* and leave the kiln door or lid ajar ½" to permit paint fumes and any possible moisture to escape. After a half hour, close the door and turn the heat to high. Keep close watch over the temperature. When the thermostat shows about 1125°F (or cone 022 bends), make sure the glass paint has become smooth and shiny; then shut off the kiln and open the vents for three minutes to halt heat rise. Finally, close the vents and let the kiln cool naturally.

Position the wooden "bridge" over the light table (or box) top. Its ends rest on the table frame. The glass is taped to the design so it can be rotated as work progresses. The design should be outlined, not drawn solid, so work can be observed as painting progresses. A 4" red sable liner makes a good brush. Paint one coat and fire it. More coats can be added.

After the first firing, thin areas will be apparent. If a perfectly opaque design is preferred, paint a second coat and fire it again.

Four small gold antique glass windows in a colonial door are painted in opaque black.

Painted owl hanging. Bette Warner.

A simple hanging made of four glass sections decorated with fired paint to create a whimsical composition. Bette Warner.

Painting on Glass—Unfired

If you want to apply a paint that does not require firing, select one of the new epoxy paints recommended for painting on glass. It is available in most large paint stores. At present, it is sold in both two-component and ready-mixed form in quarts and gallons, available in various colors. Unless you plan to use all the paint when it is first opened, it is wise to select the two-component variety and mix it in the proportions indicated on the container. Epoxy paint is prepared much like epoxy for bonding. Refer to the section "Glass Bonded with Epoxy Resin" for directions on preparation of the glass. The regular china painting #4 liner brush can be used to apply this paint. A delightful brush for applying epoxy paint in slim and curving lines is a Mack Sword Striper (from #0 on up) available in automotive supply stores.

Bonded glass and unfired epoxy paint over a rectangle of light yellow cathedral glass. The base glass is taped over the outline sketch of a bottle. Sections of colored glass spread with epoxy are pressed firmly in place. Dry overnight.

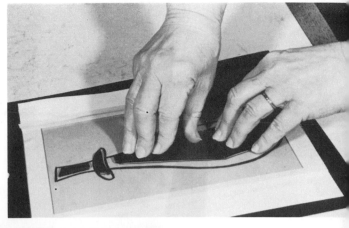

With a Mack Sword Striper brush #0, black epoxy paint is traced over the yellow glass, following the bottle sketch beneath it. The light in the table shows up the sketch clearly. Dry the paint several hours. It is not fired.

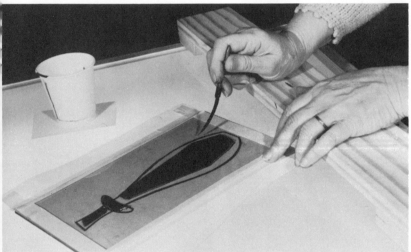

Fused Glass Wind Chimes *

Long segments of fused cathedral glass or antique stained glass with silver wire hangers make a colorful set of wind chimes that are easy to form. Cut the glass into long rectangular and triangular shapes, two for each chime. When all the planned pieces are cut out, washed, and dried, prepare 2″ lengths of fine silver wire (18-gauge) by curving the ends with small round-nosed jewelry pliers or other shaping tool. Then bend the wires double to make hanging loops for suspending the chimes. The wires will be laminated between the top ends of the glass chime layers. Brush each completed wire hanger with alcohol or acetone to remove all traces of soil which could prevent fusion.

Flat molds on which the chimes will be fused are sliced from soft

* From an article by the author that appeared in *Ceramics Monthly*.

insulation brick with a fine-toothed hacksaw. The top surface of each brick section is rubbed gently with whiting (calcium carbonate) to fill in the pores and to make a smooth surface as well as to provide a separator between the glass and the brick; it will prevent the glass from melting into the brick when the kiln is fired. Sift kiln wash over the whiting. When the glass segments, the wire hangers, and the brick sections are prepared, it is time to assemble everything ready for the kiln.

Each chime is put together on a separate section of brick. Sift clear glass flux over the *top surface* of the *bottom glass segment* of each chime and position it on a section of the prepared brick. Pick up one of the wire hangers with tweezers and position it on one end of the glass so the loop extends beyond it. You may have to hold it in place while a second glass shape, cut from the same sheet of glass, is positioned on top of the wire hanger. The edges of several of the glass chimes may be offset slightly for an interesting variation. Because the glass will only be fused, not sagged, the small offset will not slump over the edges of the glass beneath it if the heat is turned off at the indicated temperature.

If you want to fuse different glass colors together, you will probably find that some colors do not remain fused but crack apart sometime after the glass cools; the different oxides and other chemicals which determine the glass colors can result in differences in expansion and contraction as the glass heats and cools, or even when drafts in the room drift over the glass sometime after it has fired and cooled. Glasses colored with similar oxides, such as blues, greens, and turquoises, are less likely to crack apart. Colors should be test-fired before they are used in an important fused glass project.

When all the glass chimes with their wire hangers in place are assembled on the insulation bricks ready for firing, they are positioned in the cold kiln. Switches are turned to *low*. The door or lid is left open ½" to allow fumes and any kiln moisture to escape. After ½ hour of venting, the switches are turned to *high* and the vents are closed. The best way to check the progress of fused glass is to observe it visually. The differences in kilns, heating capacity, kinds and colors of glass, size of glass forms, and other factors make maturity temperatures variable. When the kiln temperature reaches 1250°F, if the edges of the glass are rounded, switches are turned off and the kiln is vented immediately to halt further heat rise. After three minutes venting, close the vent and allow the kiln to cool.

Problems arising from the firing and fusion of large glass forms are not dealt with in this book. Although shapes as small as chimes do not usually require annealing, it is wise to anneal chimes because they strike together when the wind blows them. Annealing glass is a matter of dropping the temperature at a slow controlled rate. When the kiln has been turned off, as soon as the temperature has descended as far as 950°F, turn the heat back on *low*. After ten minutes, turn it off for about ten minutes. Repeat this on and off procedure, adjusting the number of minutes heat is on and off in order to maintain a slow steady rate of temperature drop of 20° every five minutes for ⅛" thick glass, 20° every seven minutes for 3/16" glass. Glass ½" thick may require three or four hours to anneal. When the temperature has dropped to 650°F, turn the kiln heat off and let the glass cool before you remove it. Annealing relieves stresses in the glass caused by heat fusion, which makes glass brittle. In the seven years since the wind chimes illustrated here were made, none of them has cracked. Stained glass will not fuse permanently to window glass. The coefficient of expansion (rate of expansion in heating and cooling) of these two dissimilar glasses would inevitably cause cracking sometime after they cooled, or during the cooling, following removal from the kiln. If you want to achieve a fused effect, it is recommended that you fire the shapes flat, then epoxy them to a glass base; follow instructions given under "Glass Bonded with Epoxy Resin."

When the kiln has cooled completely and the chimes are removed from the bricks, some residue of whiting may cling to them; carefully sponge it off with warm water. A piece of weathered striated wood makes a support for these wind chimes whose long glass strips make a pattern of vertical striations. Colors for these chimes are blue, green, purple, and light amber. Fishline cords strung through the silver wire loops are tied to small staples driven into the back of the weathered wooden support. Touch a drop of glue to each knot to ensure it against unraveling when wind moves the chimes. The wood support can be hung with chains or leather thongs.

Slice sections of soft insulation brick to make flat molds for fusing the chimes.

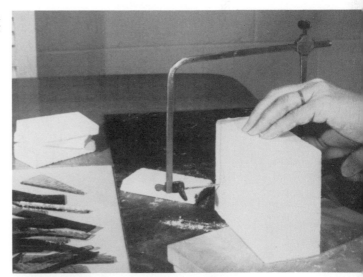

The top of each brick section is rubbed with whiting to fill pores and provide a separator between glass and brick. Sift a coat of kiln wash over it.

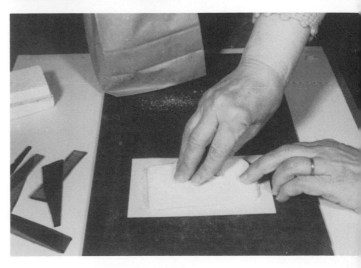

Position the wire on one end of the bottom glass piece and hold it there with tweezers while the second glass is placed on top of it.

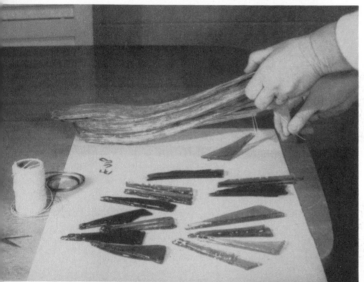

When you have fused the separate chimes in the kiln as described, they are ready to be assembled. Fishline cords strung through the wire loops are tied to small staples driven into the back of a weathered wood support.

Residue of whiting that clings to the fired glass is sponged off with warm water.

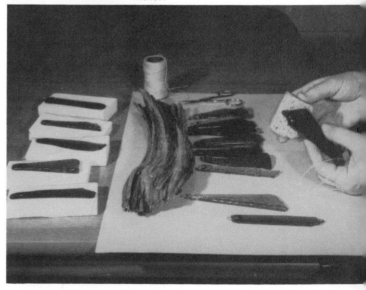

The completed wind chimes are hung with chains. Colors are blue, green, purple, and amber.

Decorative fused glass set into fences. Courtesy of the Blenko Glass Company.

Fused Stained Glass Jewelry

Contoured glass jewelry shapes can be fired in a kiln over molds formed with white ungrogged sculpture clay (cone 06). Small wire loops fused to these and other glass shapes give them great versatility as units for constructing all sorts of pieces such as bracelets, pendants, necklaces, and belts. To make the clay molds, model their top surface contours broadly shallow and their bottoms flat and level. Avoid undercuts which would prevent the release of the glass pieces when they have been fired on the molds. A tiny channel must be carved through the top of the side wall of each mold to allow air to escape when the hot glass slumps into the mold cavity. If this is neglected, a large unwanted trapped air bubble may rise under the sagging glass and distort it when the glass is fired. Dry and fire the clay molds to cone 06. When they have cooled, paint their top surfaces with whiting dissolved in water to thin cream consistency. Whiting is a separator that prevents glass from sticking to a mold when it is fired. Sift kiln wash over the whiting. Let the molds dry completely before you use them.

Cut some glass pendant shapes to match the top perimeter outlines of the small molds. Before a glass piece is positioned on a mold rim, wipe the top glass surface with a thin film of an oil such as squeegee or lavender oil (to be found in craft supply stores); sift glass *flux* in a thin layer over the oiled glass. Flux will give the glass a delicate texture and will assist the fusing process when it is fired. Position each mold with its glass pendant shape in place on a nicrome mesh firing rack. A lightweight hanger for each pendant is made of 18-gauge silver or nicrome wire bent double and shaped with its ends curled decoratively. Position it on one end of the glass pendant shape with the bent loop end of the wire extending beyond the glass. Lay a very small piece of glass on top of the wire but not covering the loop. The hanger and the small glass piece will fuse into the pendant when it is fired. For a good fusion, make sure there is some of the glass flux between the two pieces of glass. It is best to assemble the pendants on a table near the kiln to avoid the hazard of some pieces sliding to the floor when they are transported. When everything is in place, check once more to see that the hanger loops are still extending beyond the glass.

Set the firing rack into the cold kiln, which has not yet been turned on. Position it well toward the rear in a front loading kiln or near the center of the shelf in a top loading kiln. Either an enameling kiln or a ceramic kiln will fire glass satisfactorily. Turn the switch to *low* for at least a half hour with the door or lid open about one-half inch to dry out the kiln and let fumes escape as the glass warms gradually. Then close the door and turn switches to high. When the temperature reaches 1250°F (or cone 019), check to see that the little glass shapes are settling into their molds. As soon as they have settled, turn off the kiln and open the vents for three minutes to ensure that the heat rises no higher. Finally, close the vents and let the kiln cool before you remove the glass.

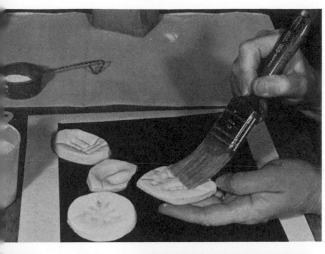

Bisqued clay molds are brushed with whiting (calcium carbonate) which acts as a separator between the clay and the glass. Sift with kiln wash.

Position glass-flux covered glass pendant shapes on clay molds. Notice the wire hangers with tiny glass pieces over them on the pendant ends.

The small glass shapes are removed from the kiln. Each glass has settled into its small mold.

The contoured shapes are decorated with Liquid Gold glass paint. Dry the gold in a warm place and fire it according to manufacturer's directions.

Completed pendants.

A Glass and Wood Bracelet

Stained glass combines beautifully with other materials. A bracelet combining links of fused stained glass with chunks of polished wood is easy to make and delightful to wear. Cut and combine the small glass shapes near the kiln to avoid dropping them in transit. The demonstration bracelet is formed with yellow stained glass and polished rosewood links. Cut small rectangles of bright yellow glass, twice as many pieces as the number of glass links you plan to use. Sift glass flux on half the links and place them on sections of insulation brick rubbed with whiting and sifted with kiln wash. On top of each glass rectangle place a silver or nicrome 18-gauge wire long enough to bend loops at each end which will extend beyond the ends of the glass piece. Cover each wire on its glass rectangle with one of the remaining glass rectangles you have cut.

Position the assemblage with its brick support on a wire mesh firing rack and insert it into the cool kiln with a firing fork. Fire it until the edges of the glass are rounded (begin checking at 1250°F). Turn the kiln off and vent it for three minutes, then close the vents and let the kiln cool completely before you remove the glass units.

To complete the bracelet, drill small holes in cut and polished rosewood pieces and join them alternately to the wire loops of the fused glass units with silver jump rings. Use regular jewelry clasps on the ends of the bracelet or make your own with silver wire or sheet. Units such as these fused glass and wire links can be combined to make all sorts of jewelry, alone or in combination with other craft materials.

Glass flux is sifted over half the glass links.

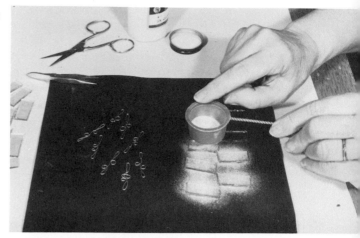

Position small wire hangers on the glass with a pair of tweezers. When each wire is covered with a second piece of glass, all pieces are placed in the kiln.

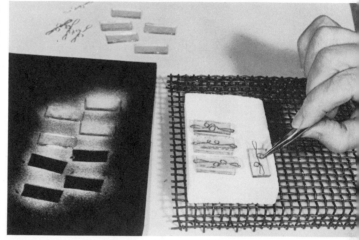

After firing, to complete the bracelet, join polished rosewood pieces (which have small holes drilled in them) to the wire loops of the fused glass units with silver jump rings.

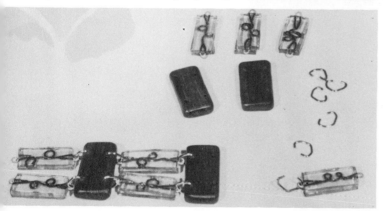

Units such as these fused links can be combined to make all sorts of jewelry, alone or combined with other materials.

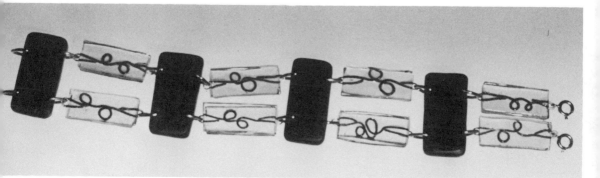

Copper Foiling

Copper foil experimentation with stained glass jewelry, hangings, and sculpture is creative and alluring. Because it is not a traditional technique, you are saved the time of breaking away from preconceived restrictions. You must strike out on your own from the beginning.

The foil is very pliable and easy to use. To attain rigidity and durability, it must be coated with solder after it is applied. Copper foil is sold in ¼" and ⅜" wide rolls 36' long, with an adhesive backing. If you use the wider nonadhesive foil, unroll it and cut off a strip about 20" long. Mark off ¼" or ⅜" intervals along each end of the strip. Lay a straightedge along the length of the foil and begin scoring with a nail or other scriber between marked intervals. With small sharp scissors, cut off *only a few strips* at a time along the scored lines; otherwise they may become a useless pile of mangled foil. Lay the strips out on paper so they do not touch one another, then spray a *thin* coat of one of the new spray adhesives over the strips. Spray the number of strips you can apply in one foiling session. When the adhesive feels tacky but not sticky, it is time to begin applying the foil.

The foil used for the demonstration project is the adhesive-backed ¼" variety. The glass is broken slab glass segments. Narrow ready-coated foil has a strip of paper backing that is peeled away as you apply the foil to a glass edge. It is imperative to keep both the glass and the foil clean and free of skin oil, so after it is cleaned handle it gingerly. Brush it with a very fine copper brush to remove oxidation. Alcohol or acetone will clean off oil.

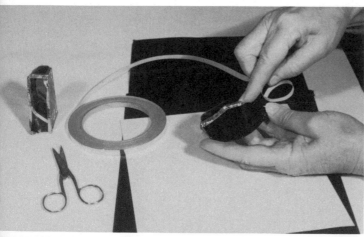

Pick up a clean glass piece as lightly as possible to keep skin oil from soiling it. Peel off some paper backing and press the narrow copper foil along a glass ridge.

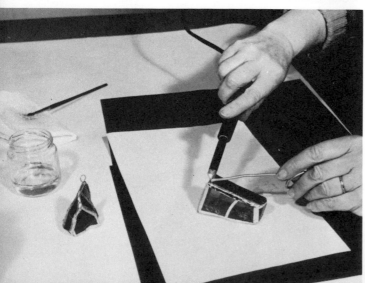

Press it firmly into all crevices; solder the foil ends together. Apply soldering flux and run solder over the entire copper area. Twisted wire hangers are soldered in place.

Completed copper foiled hangings from slab glass segments.

Glass Sculpture. Jean Abbott. Four three-dimensional stained glass pyramidal shapes foiled and soldered together. 12 inches tall. Photo by Alden Abbott.

Once the foil and glass are clean, pick up a glass piece, peel away some paper backing, and wrap the foil along a glass ridge so that an equal amount of foil is pressed to each side. Press it firmly into all crevices and cut off the foil strip so it fits flush with the starting end. Apply soldering flux (oleic acid) to the copper ends and solder them together. If the solder does not cling to the copper, it may be soiled or the iron may not be hot enough. Because the melting point of copper is much higher than that of tin or lead, it is not easily melted. Apply a few foil strips in different directions over the glass lump along its ridges, then cover them generously with 60/40 solid core solder to create a firm cage around the glass (don't forget the flux!). If you plan to hang the foiled glass, solder a 16-gauge copper wire hanger to it. For intriguing small sculptures, solder some *foiled glass chunks* together and epoxy them to a base. The solder-covered foiled edges of *sheet glass units* can be fitted together and soldered to make beautiful lamps and sculptures as well.

5 * Combining Techniques

STAINED GLASS is a delightful and exciting medium for craftsmen of all ages. Although a form may be simple, the moment sunlight floods through it, brilliant shimmering color delights the eye. Pieces of contrasting bonded colored glass and even fused crushed glass sparkle and glow. Provide a subtle layered effect with small shapes fused to glass that will be bonded or leaded. Add an exotic touch to dull leads by rubbing metallic paste finishes over them to transform them with rich coloring. The projects illustrated here show several techniques combined into complex compositions. For an exciting way to create with glass, make use of a variety of methods to put bits of color wherever you want them.

Small Window Panels

Glass for a small leaded window panel is spread out on the light table for a final check of color relationships. The separate glass piece that has been removed from the composition will be painted and fired before it is leaded.

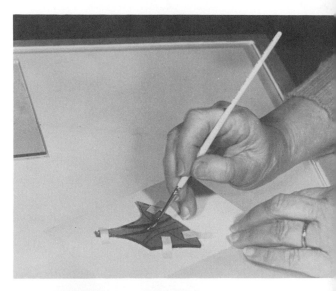

The glass piece is taped to a design over the light table so it can be revolved as painting progresses. A wood bridge is not needed for this one glass piece.

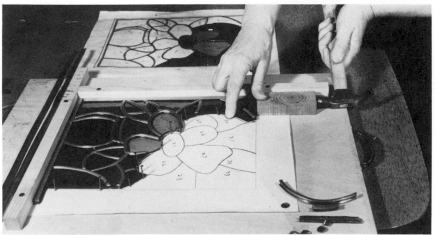

A complex design with irregularly shaped pieces must be braced securely with one hand while the glass is tapped firmly into position in the lead. Otherwise pieces will slide out of place when they are tapped with the wood block. Geometric compositions are easier to control.

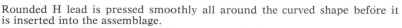

Rounded H lead is pressed smoothly all around the curved shape before it is inserted into the assemblage.

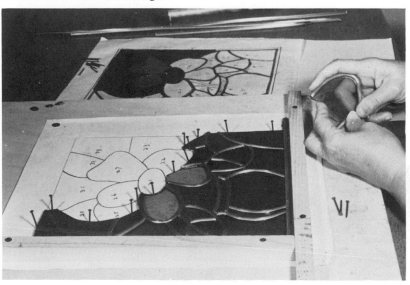

When the panel is completely leaded and soldered on both sides, the glass is cleaned thoroughly to remove oil from the oleic acid. Several small glass shapes are epoxied into place for a sparkling effect. It is wise to wear gloves when you use epoxy products. Avoid inhaling the fumes.

The panel gleams with color against the sunlit snow. It is puttied into place against the regular window glass.

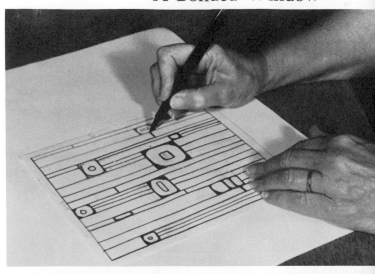

A small-scale sketch for a bonded window, "Stems and Flowers." Dark areas will be black grout.

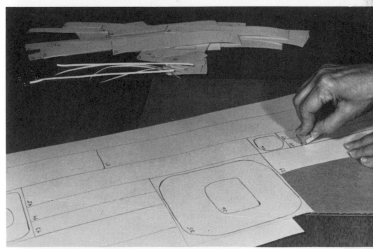

Three copies are made of the full-scale drawing. Only one border line is required for the cartoon and copies of a bonded window.

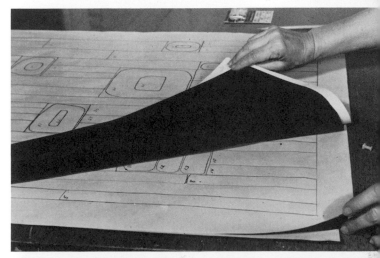

Patterns are cut out with a double razor-bladed tool.

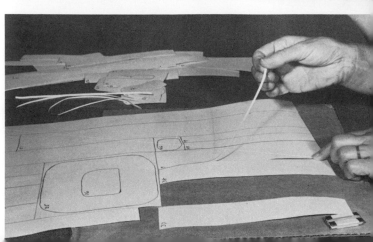

Removing the strips which indicate spaces where grouting will be applied instead of leading.

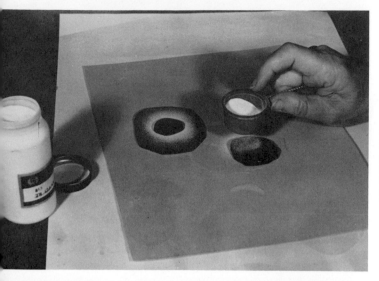

The abstract flower shapes will be fused and bonded, both singly and in layers. To facilitate fusion, sift flux over the glass before it is fired. (For directions on fusing small pieces refer to the section "Fused Glass Wind Chimes.")

It is advisable to read again the instructions under "Glass Bonded with Epoxy Resin" before you begin work on a large project. This window is bonded in four sessions. Only one-fourth of the total amount of glass in this window can be bonded before the epoxy resin begins to set, if only one person is bonding. Masking tape along the edge *must* be removed as soon as the epoxy in each section becomes rubbery.

The third application begins. It is important to keep hands and any soil or dust off the areas of glass that will be epoxied. Success in a bonded project depends on meticulous crafting.

A section of the bonded window, "Stems and Flowers." Polly Rothenberg. Designed for and installed in the home of Mr. and Mrs. James Martin.

Pendant. Polly Rothenberg. Crushed glass fused to enameled hand-formed and contoured copper pendant. Handmade links.*

Bonded crushed glass in a ceramic table lamp. Laura Dunn.

A Large Butterfly Hanging

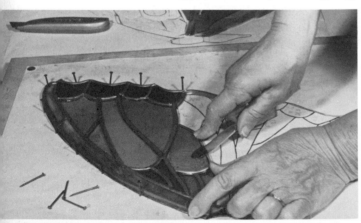

Leading for a large stained glass butterfly begins at the border of the top right wing and progresses down the panel.

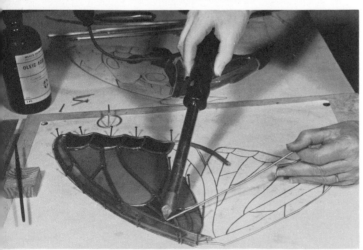

Leading along each side of wing sections is continuous; it is soldered together at each wing tip. After every two or three glass pieces are inserted, they are tapped securely into the lead and soldered.

*See Metal Enameling by Polly Rothenberg. Crown Publishers Arts and Crafts Series.

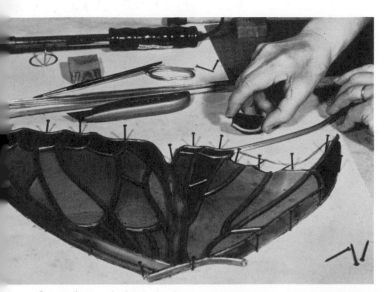

One piece of lead is bent around two sides of each border scalloped piece before it is inserted into the border leading.

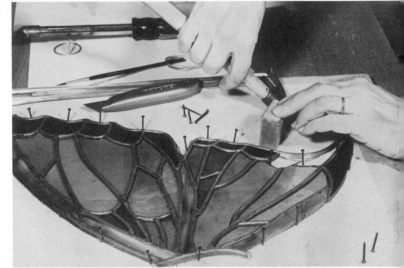

Tap each piece firmly so it lines up with the drawn design underneath it.

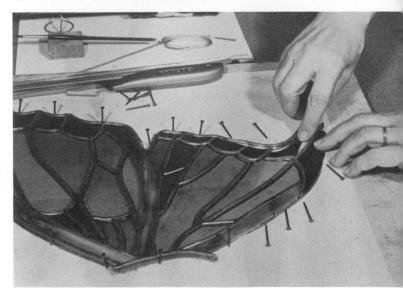

Final wing pieces are inserted. Notice that some of the nails are removed so border leads can be fitted.

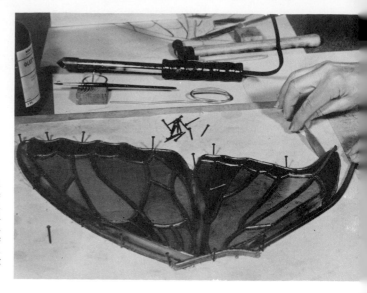

The last lead is fitted along a wing edge. Glass shapes are worked into the leading with the small knife. An end of lead is left extending ½" long at each wing tip and is curved to give decorative effect and to provide a hanging hook at each upper wing tip.

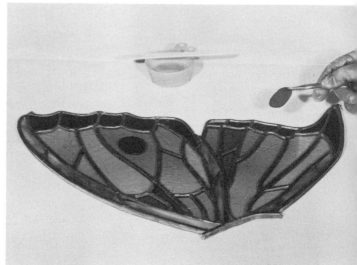

After the glass has been thoroughly cleaned, wing spots are epoxied into position. The epoxy is dried completely. Finally, the wing is turned over and soldered at each joint. The leads are puttied to give added firmness to the composition. Scrub away the soil and putty with whiting as described earlier. A second wing is prepared in reverse, identical to the first.

A hammered, contoured copper body is made in two sections. Brush 40/60 low fusing paste solder along the edges of each half, inside and outside. Bind them securely with regular jeweler's binding wire around the head and tail and insert the body into the leading of the wings where they normally join the body.

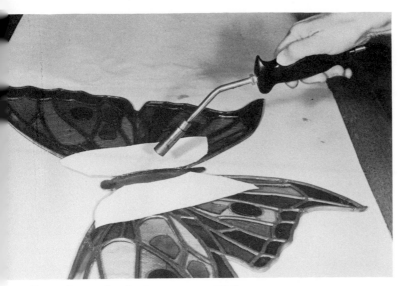

Two pieces of asbestos paper protect glass and lead while a propane torch applies the low heat required to melt this solder.

Achieve a final rich effect on any of your leaded stained glass creations by rubbing the leads and solder with any of the nontoxic lustrous metallic paste finishes. They come in dozens of beautiful metallic colors. The butterfly leading is covered with bronze wax paste. The antennae are made from doubled wire soldered to the copper head with 40/60 solder.

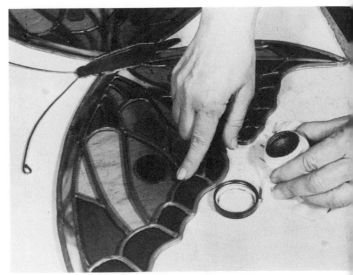

The completed butterfly is 26" from wing tip to wing tip. It is 16" deep. It can be made strong by soldering slender steel rods on the back side, that cross the body diagonally behind the opalescent edges of the wings. Or it can be suspended in a framework of slender metal rods. This butterfly is adequately supported with very fine steel wires that suspend it from the small lead "hooks" at the tips of the upper wings. Very light blue glass over most of the butterfly gives it a fragile gossamer character, for such a large composition. Additional colors are deep blue, green, orange, and lavender.

Bibliography

Duval, Jean-Jacques. *Working with Stained Glass*. New York: Thomas Y. Crowell Company, 1972.

Isenberg, Anita and Seymour. *How to Work in Stained Glass*. New York, Philadelphia, and London: Chilton Book Company, 1972.

Koch, Robert. *Louis C. Tiffany, Rebel in Glass*. New York: Crown Publishers, Inc., 1964.

Metcalf, Robert and Gertrude. *Making Stained Glass*. New York: McGraw Hill Book Company, 1972.

Reyntiens, Patrick. *The Techniques of Stained Glass*. New York: Watson-Guptill Publications, 1967.

Rothenberg, Polly. *Metal Enameling*. New York: Crown Publishers, Inc., 1969.

Stribling, Mary Lou. *Mosaic Techniques*. New York: Crown Publishers, Inc., 1966.

Periodicals: *Ceramics Monthly*, Columbus, Ohio; *Craft Horizons*, New York City; *Stained Glass Quarterly*, St. Louis, Missouri (published by Stained Glass Association of America).

Supply Sources

Adhesive Spray for Copper Foil

3M—Minnesota Mining & Manufacturing Company
St. Paul, Minnesota 55119

Copper Trays for Lantern Tops, Copper Foil

Allcraft Tool & Supply Company
215 Park Avenue
Hicksville, New York 11801

American Metalcraft Company
4100 Belmont Avenue
Chicago, Illinois 60641

Epoxy Systems, Cements and Compounds

Benesco Company
40 North Rock Hill
St. Louis, Missouri 63119

H & M Plastics Corporation
129 South Second Street
Philadelphia, Pennsylvania 19106

Thermoset Plastics, Incorporated
5101 East 65th Street
Indianapolis, Indiana 46220

General Supplies

Tepping Studio Supply Company
3003 Salem Avenue
Dayton, Ohio 45406

Glass, Antique, Rondels, Dalles

Blenko Glass Company
Milton, West Virginia 25541

Glass, Cathedral Glass

Advance Glass Company
Newark, Ohio 43055

Kokomo Opalescent Glass Company
1310 South Market Street
Kokomo, Indiana 46901

Glass Paints, Fired

B. F. Drakenfeld & Company
45 Park Place
New York, New York 10007

Whittemore-Durgin Glass Company
Box 2065 FA
Hanover, Mass. 02339

L. Reusche & Company
2 Lister Avenue
Newark, New Jersey 07105

Standard Ceramic Supply Company
P.O. Box 4435
Pittsburgh, Pennsylvania 15205

Thomas C. Thompson Company
1539 Old Deerfield Road
Highland Park, Illinois 60035

Glass Paints, Unfired

Fuller O'Brien Corporation
South San Francisco, California
  94080
(Write for nearest dealer name and
  a color chart)

Mira Plate Epoxy Paint
The O'Brien Corporation
South Bend, Indiana 46628

Glazing Compound (Dap "33 Gray")

Dap, Incorporated
5300 Huberville Road
Dayton, Ohio 45431

Grout and Grout Colorants

Technical Adhesives
Division of H. B. Fuller Company
315 South Hicks Road
Palatine, Illinois 60067

Knives, Lead Cutting

S. Camlott
520 Hollywood Avenue
Salt Lake City, Utah 84105

Matt Knives

Obtainable at artist supply stores

Metallic Antique Colored Paste Finishes for Lead

"La Tip," Leo Uhlfelder Company
New York, New York 10001

"Rub-N-Buff," American Art Clay
  Company
4717 West 16th Street
Indianapolis, Indiana 46222

"Treasure Jewels," Connoisseur
  Studio
Louisville, Kentucky 40207

Pattern Scissors

S. A. Bendheim Company,
  Incorporated
122 Hudson Street
New York, New York 10013

Index